T0374542

Peacebuilding After Peace Accords:
The Challenges of Violence, Truth, and Youth

Tristan Anne Borer, John Darby, and Siobhán McEvoy-Levy

Peacebuilding After Peace Accords:
The Challenges of Violence, Truth, and Youth

Tristan Anne Borer, John Darby, and Siobhán McEvoy-Levy

University of Notre Dame Press

Copyright © 2006 by University of Notre Dame
Notre Dame, Indiana 46556
www.undpress.nd.edu
All Rights Reserved

Library of Congress Cataloging in-Publication Data

Borer, Tristan Anne, 1965-
   Peacebuilding after peace accords : the challenges of violence, truth and youth / Tristan Anne Borer, John Darby, and Siobhán McEvoy-Levy.
   p. cm.—(RIREC project on post-accord peacebuilding)
   Includes bibliographical references.
   ISBN-13: 978-0-268-02204-4 (pbk.)
   ISBN-10: 0-268-02204-6 (pbk.)
   1. Peacebuilding. I. Darby, John. II. McEvoy-Levy, Siobhán, 1968- III. Title.
   JZ5538.B66 2006
   327.1'72-dc22

                              2006028618

The paper in this book meets the guidelines for permanence and durability of the Committee on Production Guidelines for Book Longevity of the Council on Library Resources.

On the cover: Officials in the Philippines celebrate the first anniversary of the peace agreement between the government and Misuari's Moro National Liberation Front in a 1997 photo by Bullit Marquez; and Catholic children play with toy guns under an Irish Republican Army mural in the South Belfast, Northern Ireland, in a 2001 photo by Peter Morrison.

For John, Marie, and Andy

CONTENTS

FOREWORD

The Struggle for Social Justice in Post-apartheid South Africa
Archbishop Emeritus Desmond Mpilo Tutu

In 2004 we celebrate a decade of freedom and democracy in South Africa, commemorating that wholly unexpected and quite spectacular victory over one of the world's most vicious political systems and the relatively peaceful transition from repression to freedom in 1994.

Who will ever easily forget those long, long lines of South Africans of every race winding their way slowly to the polling booths on that magical, not-to-be-forgotten day, April 27, 1994? Many had predicted that South Africa would be overwhelmed by the most awful racial bloodbath. It did not happen. We are the beneficiaries of much love and commitment and fervent prayer by millions in the international community. People had boycotted South African goods on our behalf, they had demonstrated and held rallies for us, and many were arrested on our behalf. We can never thank you enough. I can, without being presumptuous, say I know I speak on behalf of millions of my compatriots when I say to you all, "Thank you, thank you, thank you." We are able to say we will be celebrating ten years of freedom and democracy because of you. We are free today because of you; we are striving to be democratic, to be nonracial and nonsexist because of you. It is a debt we will never be able to repay.

Most expected that once a black-led government was installed, then South Africa would see an orgy of retribution and revenge as blacks went on the rampage giving vent to all their pent-up fury for all those many, many years when they suffered untold misery all because of their ethnicity, their race, their skin color. One of the songs of our struggle is a haunting melody that asks plaintively in Xhosa, "Zenzenina?" ("What have we done? Our sin is our blackness.")

Yes, that was the conventional expectation, that the post-conflict period would be a time of reckoning. Instead, the world was awed by the spectacle of the Truth and Reconciliation process when victims of frequently gruesome atrocities revealed a mind-boggling nobility and generosity of spirit in their

Comments delivered at the opening event of the RIREC conference on Post-Accord Peacebuilding at the University of Notre Dame, Notre Dame, IN, September 2003. Desmond Mpilo Tutu is Anglican Archbishop Emeritus of Cape Town, South Africa and the winner of the 1984 Nobel Peace Prize.

magnanimous willingness to forgive the perpetrator. We rejected the twin options of a type of Nuremberg trial and the general amnesia of blanket amnesty. We resolved to look the beast in the eye, to let victims tell their story, to risk opening wounds which had seemed to have healed when they were in reality festering. We opened those wounds, cleansed them, and poured on them the balm of acknowledgement, of giving voice to hurt, of rehabilitating the dignity of those who for so long were anonymous, faceless victims. Perpetrators were given the chance to come to terms with what they had done, to make a full disclosure, and then to obtain amnesty in an example of restorative justice which was more about healing than about punishment, more about forgiveness and reconciliation than about retribution and revenge.

We knew that none of us possesses a fiat—we are not God—so that bygones would be bygones. We knew that the deeds of the past had an uncanny capacity to return and haunt people. The TRC [Truth and Reconciliation Commission] was a way of hope, of faith in the fundamental goodness of people, that we would not give up on anyone, that even the worst perpetrator still remained a child of God with the capacity to change, that each of us has the capacity to become a saint.

Forgiveness and reconciliation have been shown not to be nebulous, namby-pamby things. No, they are the stuff of realpolitik. The alternative, the way of revenge, of retribution, leads to a ghastly cul-de-sac—the spiral of reprisal-provoking counter reprisal ad infinitum, ending with no security, no peace, but a toll in human lives and property that is inexorable and exorbitant. It is not to be merely idealistic to say that without forgiveness there is no future; it is being a hard-nosed realist. Just ask the people of the Middle East and of Northern Ireland or Sri Lanka or Rwanda. True peace and real security will never come from the barrel of a gun, however overwhelming. Peace and security come because all enjoy justice and freedom. Peace and security come because it is acknowledged that people matter.

Social Justice in Post-Apartheid South Africa

Apartheid was vicious, having refined the racism that had been part and parcel of the South African way of life from the moment white people encountered the indigenous people of that part of the continent. It was a policy of exclusion. The vast majority of the people were excluded from all real political decision making, which gave access to all other kinds of power, rights, and resources. We were talked about; we were legislated for and about. They, the powerful, hardly talked to us and yet you could say most of the work of Parliament, indeed all of white politics, had to do with how do you deal with the natives, the blacks, "those" people. Whites-only elections were won by the party that demonstrated that it knew how to keep the black properly in his place. And so you had the Pass Laws which restricted black movement severely in the land of their birth. Blacks were temporary sojourners in so-called white South Africa, so there was no point in building houses for them in those urban areas. Do you see what I am trying to establish? That almost all our problems are a legacy, the ghastly legacy, of apartheid. Of course, many have since been exacerbated by what we have subsequently decided would be public policy. It is not looking for a convenient scapegoat—it is so that we will make a realistic assessment of our situation and prescribe appropriate remedies.

If you don't build houses then you should not be surprised that there will be a horrendous backlog. When influx control is lifted, then those who were locked in the poverty-stricken homelands will stream to the cities whose streets, it is fondly imagined from time immemorial, are lined with gold. So we should not be surprised at all the so-called informal settlements that have mushroomed all over the place in our country.

The migratory labor system played havoc with black family life when the father alone was allowed into the white area to lead an unnatural life in a single-sex hostel, prey to drunkenness, prostitution, drugs and, other antisocial conduct whilst his family—whom he would not see for nine to twelve months—eked out a miserable existence in the arid, under-resourced rural area. The white Dutch Reformed Church, which at the time provided theological justification for apartheid, had castigated this system as a cancer. There was a Population Registration Act according to which the population of our country was branded like so many animals. The methods to determine race were often crude and unscientific, like sticking a pin unexpectedly in the victim and assigning a race label according to his shriek of pain, or by putting a comb through his hair. Sometimes siblings were assigned to different race groups because one was of a darker hue than others. Children sometimes committed suicide when this happened, for whiteness was the open sesame to massive privilege and benefit. There was a Prohibition of Mixed Marriages Act, which prohibited marriage between whites and people of other races, and the Immorality Act, which prohibited sexual relations between whites and people of other races. People committed suicide for being accused under this legislation. It made sordid something that should have been beautiful and noble—love between two people.

By law blacks were confined to owning only 13 percent of the land while comprising 80 percent of the population. The remaining 87 percent of the land was enjoyed by 20 percent of the people: whites. The apartheid government spent on a white child's education nearly ten times per annum what it spent on a black child. This inequity was compounded by the introduction of Bantu education, which was deliberately inferior: nothing about even the fiction of "separate but equal." They knew they were fobbing off our children with an inferior and poisonous gruel designed to turn them into docile, kowtowing, perpetual serfs. After all, prime minister Dr Verwoerd made no bones about the aims of Bantu Education. He maintained that there was no point in teaching blacks mathematics; let them know enough English and Afrikaans to be able to understand the instructions of their white boss and missus. He was unashamedly forthright. Our children, wonderfully, rejected what they called "gutter education" in the Soweto uprising of June 16, 1976. Education through high school was free for whites and not for blacks, who were often not able to afford it.

It was the same in every sphere of life. The Job Reservation Act prohibited blacks from performing certain skilled work and now you hear whites bleating about affirmative action. Our country had pioneered the first heart transplant, showing we were up there with the best in sophisticated medical technology, but people were dying of cholera simply through a lack of clean water—we have to add that the people referred to were of course black people. Hardly any whites died of cholera. They had readier access to very adequate medical care. Black people, especially in the rural areas, trudged long distances to rivers to collect often-polluted river water and chopped down trees for fuel, so encouraging soil erosion. In the meantime, wires bearing electricity passed over these farm areas. In addition to all this was the daily grind of being humiliated and treated as something to be spoken of in the third person, a non-European, a non-white, a non-entity. It did not take long from being spoken of as a non-entity to being treated as nothing, as not counting for much. Sadly, devastatingly, it did not take long for many so treated to think of themselves as non-entities, with a sense of self-hatred gnawing at the very vitals of one's being causing us to doubt that we too were God's children. The utter blasphemy of it all, almost to spit in the face of God. Ja—when you look back on it, you have to say the magnanimity of those made to suffer so was truly magnificent. They had every reason to want to pay back in the same coin. *Ubuntu* prevented it—they knew that their humanity was caught up in the humanity of the other—that we were created for family, for togetherness, for sharing, for existing in a delicate network of interdependence, and hatred and anger and revenge were corrosive of this *summum bonus*, the greater good of communal harmony.

How one wishes there were a magic wand which one could wave and, "Hey presto," all the awfulness would be changed into its glorious counterpart. We have set ourselves high and noble goals in the new South Africa, but it is going to take us a long while to attain them without substantial help from our allies in the international community. Our Constitution entitles every South African to a decent home, to adequate health care, to a good education, to the so-called economic, cultural, and social rights and our highest court, the Constitutional Court, has declared that they are enforceable—they are not just nice ideals to strive after. It has given two particularly significant judgments: that government, within reason, must provide its citizens with decent housing, and it found in favor of those who were demanding antiretroviral treatment for people living with HIV/AIDS. So they are not just theoretical rights ensconced in a paper constitution. People can sue the government if they think they are being denied their constitutional rights enshrined, in our case, in the Bill of Rights at the beginning of our Constitution.

We frequently celebrate what people elsewhere take so very much for granted, the arrival of clean piped water to a previously deprived community. The authorities have set a target of a quarter of a million houses to be constructed per annum. Education is universally free to the end of high school but it is a right determined by availability of resources, and health care is free up to the age of six years and for expectant mothers; concentration is on primary health-care with the building of clinics, especially in the rural areas. We are being overwhelmed by the devastating HIV/AIDS pandemic. Wonderfully, though most of the victims are black, it is heartwarming to see just how many whites are working assiduously to combat this scourge.

We have seen in Zimbabwe what can happen when the vexed question of land possession is not dealt with expeditiously and carefully. Our government is following an orderly and legal method to restore land to its former dispossessed owners in its land restitution programs.

Women are coming more and more into their own. We are striving to be gender-sensitive and we have many splendid women, especially in the public sector, but there is no room for complacency. We face enormous problems posed by poverty, crime, disease, and corruption. In our Truth and Reconciliation Commission Report we declared that unless the gap between the rich and the poor, the haves and have nots, was reduced drastically we could just as well kiss reconciliation goodbye. In many ways we are sitting on a powder keg. I am still amazed at the patience of our people. Many, far too many, still live in squalor, poverty, and deprivation, in shacks without running water or electricity. Every day they wake up early in the morning to take a crowded train, bus, or taxi to town, to the salubrious, affluent suburbs whose citizens are still largely white (not exclusively now) with beautiful, well-built homes, with all the mod cons—and they are the domestic workers, the cooks, the cleaners, the child-minders, the gardeners, the drivers, all who make it possible for the wealthy to work—and in the evening they leave all that to return to their squalor and poverty. I have wondered when they will get incensed and lose their patience and say to hell with Madiba [Nelson Mandela] and Tutu with their reconciliation, and go on the rampage. We have said to our white compatriots that transformation of the physical, material circumstances of these deprived ones is not altruism. It is the best form of self-interest. It is so globally. We are unlikely to win the war against terrorism as long as there are conditions which make people so desperate because of their poverty, of their deprivation, their illnesses, their lack of security, etc.—making them so desperate that they are ready to commit acts of terrorism.

It is in our best interests in South Africa and everywhere to try to achieve the eight goals of the Millennium Plan: to halve poverty (we should eradicate it in South Africa), to provide free education, to make health care readily available to all, to reduce infant mortality, to advance the cause of women, to deal with AIDS, TB, and malaria, to remove slums, and to develop global partnership for development. I think we are doing well but we can do better. But we really cannot do this without your help.

A Kind of Marshall Plan

Western Europe was devastated by World War II. To help Europe get back on its feet the United States provided help through the Marshall Plan. Southern Africa, not just South Africa, has been devastated by apartheid. I think a case could be made for a special Marshall Plan-type of aid to help us deal with the ghastly legacy of apartheid.

I am not greedy. The U.S. gives over US$3 billion to Israel per annum because, rightly, the continued existence of Israel is important for the world—we hope for an Israel that would live in peace with its neighbors, including a viable, independent, and sovereign Palestinian state.

I think a successful, vibrant South Africa is equally important for the world as an experiment in coexistence of different races, of former oppressors and oppressed in a post-conflict land. So I would urge that an annual grant of US$2 billion for five years be granted to us to deal with the legacy of apartheid. It could even be earmarked and designated for certain projects only—health, education, and housing. It would be a most worthwhile investment. You helped us to become free. Help us to become successful, for we are, very oddly, totally improbably, a beacon of hope for the rest of the world—if it could happen in South Africa, it can happen any and everywhere. Peace and stability are possible in the post-conflict period.

PREFACE

Peacebuilding After Peace Accords is the capstone volume to the first phase of a multiyear, multidisciplinary research project directed by John Darby, professor of comparative ethnic studies at the Joan B. Kroc Institute for International Peace Studies, University of Notre Dame. The project, known in these halls as the Research Initiative on the Resolution of Ethnic Conflict (RIREC), analyzes the implementation of more than thirty peace accords that have been negotiated and signed by parties to ethnic, political, resource, religious, and civil wars around the world since the end of the Cold War. The ultimate goal of the project is to evaluate the various efforts at implementation of peace accords, account for the successes and failures, discern and identify patterns and obstacles, and eventually formulate lessons and recommendations for policymakers, diplomats, negotiators, and other interested parties to the protracted conflicts that bedevil their host nations and often implicate distant states and other international actors.

The second phase of RIREC, currently under way, is devoted to building a data base, known colloquially as "the Matrix," which will provide to an internet-connected, geographically dispersed professional community of conflict mediators and peacebuilders a considerable amount of information and analysis of previous and ongoing peace processes during their various phases of design and implementation. Armed with this comparative data, peacemakers in locales as far apart as, say, Sri Lanka, Northern Ireland, and Colombia, it is hoped, will be better prepared to apply the relevant "lessons learned" to their particular situations.

The present volume offers a reflection on and synthesis of the findings of three scholarly volumes published in 2006 by the University of Notre Dame Press and, more broadly, of the insights obtained from the authors' own years of research into peace processes, enhanced by the numerous meetings, conversations, and individual communications they enjoyed with an array of colleagues. From 2000 to 2003, the RIREC initiative drew on the expertise of dozens of authorities in the field, commissioning many of them to attend Kroc Institute-hosted workshops, deliver draft chapters at an international conference held at Notre Dame in 2003, and then polish and publish these original accounts of their experiences and studies of peace processes. Specifically, three teams of scholars identified and integrated the study of three key dimensions of the post-accord landscape: post-accord violence, the role of young people in violent conflict and peacebuilding, and truth telling and peacebuilding.

Each research cluster produced an edited book. Professor Darby edited a volume of essays devoted to the theme of *Violence and Reconstruction.* Professor Tristan Anne Borer of Connecticut College led the team that examined *Telling the Truths: Truth Telling and Peace Building in Post-Conflict Societies.* Professor Siobhán McEvoy-Levy of Butler University edited the volume that focused on *Troublemakers and Peacemakers: Youth and Post-Accord Peace Building.* Separately, each of these topics engages conflict management and conflict trans-formation challenges and opportunities. The synergy between youth, truth telling, and transitional justice, and post-accord violence, however, had not been conceptualized in this fashion, much less systematically studied as a dynamic process generating its own outcomes and patterns of behavior. Yet any peace process is doomed to failure, Professor Darby has argued, if it lacks a realistic strategy to reduce levels of violence and counterviolence; if it skirts the hard political, legal, and cultural choices that nurture genuine reconciliation; and if it fails to recognize and accommodate the central role of youth. Together, the series of three books develops new perspectives on post-accord peacebuilding, as well as on the intersections between different aspects of reconstruction that were once studied in isolation.

While there is no substitute for mastering—and citing—the trio of edited volumes, specialists in international affairs, peace and conflict studies, foreign policy, and related disciplines will want to linger even longer over the insights and candid evaluations presented in *Peacebuilding After Peace Accords.* Not least, students and the educated general public will profit from this sustained reflec-tion on the dilemmas and trends in postwar reconstruction and the challenges to building a sustainable peace in societies recently riven by deadly violence. Indeed, this succinct and eloquent book will engage fruitfully anyone concerned about the interrelated challenges of internecine bloodshed, state-sponsored vio-lence, the proliferation of militant youth gangs and movements, the thorny problem of coming to terms with the human rights violations of the past, and the largely unsatisfying aftermath of most, if not all, peace accords attempted over the past several years.

R. Scott Appleby
Professor of History
John M. Regan Jr. Director, Joan B. Kroc Institute for International Peace Studies
University of Notre Dame

ACKNOWLEDGEMENTS

This research was funded in part by the Joan B. Kroc Institute for International Peace Studies at the University of Notre Dame, the United States Institute of Peace (USIP), and the Fulbright New Century Scholars Program. The authors are grateful for this support.

In addition, we wish to express our gratitude to the following individuals and organizations:

- Tristan Anne Borer is grateful to Mark Freeman of the International Center for Transitional Justice (ICTJ) for helpful organizational insights, to John Nugent for reading, commenting on, and editing portions of this manuscript, and the Office of the Dean of the Faculty at Connecticut College for sabbatical support.
- John Darby is grateful to Thomas Pettigrew, Roger Mac Ginty, Mirak Raheem, Irene Zirimwabagabo, and Dominic Murray for their responses to earlier drafts of portions of this research.
- Siobhán McEvoy-Levy is grateful to Jeffrey Helsing and Andrew Levy for their comments on drafts of sections of this book and to colleagues at Butler University, especially Robert Holm of University Research Programs, for financial support.

CHAPTER 1

The Post-Accord Landscape:
New Challenges and New Responses

A new type of peace process, one primarily driven by internal negotiators, emerged during the 1990s. It looked to contemporary rather than
to historical cases for approaches to peacemaking, and reflected an
optimism that international violence, expressed through Cold War tensions, was in decline. In 1991 and 1992 the number of interstate and
intrastate armed conflicts exceeded fifty. This number had diminished
to thirty or under by 2003 and 2004.[1] Most of the decline was the
result of negotiations leading to peace agreements.

It is not easy to classify these peace agreements. Definitions and
methods of classification vary. Even if one concentrates on agreements
that might be described as comprehensive,[2] as opposed to literally hundreds of partial agreements, the total is impressive. The Peace Matrix
project at Notre Dame[3] calculates that between 1989 and 2001 comprehensive peace agreements were signed in more than twenty-six
countries, and at least eight more have been negotiated since 2001;
almost all were between combatants previously engaged in violent
internal conflicts. The Conflict Data Project at the University of
Uppsala classified forty six comprehensive peace agreements between
1889 and 2004[4] and the United States Institute of Peace (USIP) details
forty comprehensive agreements between 1989 and 2005,[5] including
fifteen in Africa, eleven in Asia, seven in Europe, five in the Americas,
and two in the Middle East. The geographical pattern is similar in the
other two data sets.

Have they led to stability? Peace agreements do not lend themselves to easy classification along a spectrum between failure and success. The return to open violence is a clear indication of failure. It is
much more difficult to point to unqualified success, or even to define
what might constitute success. As Oliver Richmond puts it,
"Contemporary approaches to creating peace, from first generation
conflict management approaches to third generation peace-building
approaches, rarely stop to imagine the kind of peace they may actually

create, or question the conceptualization inherent in their deployment."[6] Local actors often present a much more pessimistic audit of progress than external observers. The problem is that, in many cases, war has not been succeeded by peace but by a no-war, no-peace stalemate, harried by intermittent violence, economic struggle, crime, persistent suspicion, and public dissatisfaction.

So, despite the growth in peacemaking, the euphoria of the 1990s has not survived into the new century. Some peace processes have progressed, but many have collapsed and others have failed to fulfill their early promise. Agreements signed in Israel/Palestine (1994), Colombia (1999), Eritrea-Ethiopia (2000), and elsewhere have collapsed into violent confrontation. Even in South Africa, Guatemala, and El Salvador, often regarded as among the countries with the most enduring peace agreements, recovery has been undermined by high crime and low economic growth, stemming in part from the preceding violence. Eight years after the Good Friday Agreement, Northern Ireland still experiences stalemate, and a power-sharing administration seems a distant prospect. So the main reason for applying more attention to the dynamics of post-agreement implementation, reconciliation, and reconstruction is clear. The completion of a peace accord marks the start of another phase in a peace process and, perhaps, another phase in conflict.

The Academic Response

Academic research hunts at the heels of emerging international problems, and the peace processes of the 1990s attracted significant academic attention. Initially many of the studies concentrated on single cases, with the Oslo process for Israel/Palestine and the Northern Ireland peace negotiations producing a particularly high volume of research and commentary.[7] The transition to democracy in South Africa has also received much attention in the peace process literature.[8] Other peace initiatives, in Mindanao or Guinea-Bissau, for example, have received considerably less attention. As the 1990s progressed, comparative studies began to benefit from the simultaneous existence of a growing number of peace processes. Doyle, Johnstone, and Orr have described the changes in multi-dimensional peacekeeping in Cambodia and El Salvador, primarily from a UN perspective.[9] Hampson's 1996 study of five peace settlements, all with UN involvement, singled out the role of third parties and emphasized the importance of post-accord implementation.[10] The comparative studies by Darby and Mac Ginty, which broadened the canvas to include cases with no UN involvement, highlighted the complexity of different approaches necessary as peace processes move from violence into negotiations, and from peace agreements to reconstruction.[11]

Substantial bodies of research have coalesced around certain themes, notably the origins and dynamics of ethnic violence, the first moves towards negotiations, and spoiler violence. Gurr[12] and Geller and Singer[13] have analyzed patterns of violence during the twentieth century and since. Others, notably

Harbom and Wallensteen[14] and the International Research Program on Root Causes of Human Rights Violations (PIOOM),[15] have charted the changing patterns in contemporary violence throughout the world, and have updated them on a regular basis. As a result of these and other studies, we have a much more detailed understanding of how global violence has changed since the end of the Cold War, most notably away from international war and towards internal violence. Initially, a major concern for many scholars was how entry points may be found in the conflict cycle for external intervention. Zartman[16] and Haass[17] emphasized the importance of taking advantage of the "ripe moment" when the parties in conflict have reached a "hurting stalemate"—when the costs and prospects of war outweigh the costs and prospects of settlement for the major combatants. Despite the understandable focus on violence, it is still remarkable that the dominant message from research on peace processes is that modern wars are more likely to terminate at the negotiating table than on the battlefield.[18]

Research approaches have become more sophisticated, mirroring the broadening of peace processes beyond security and constitutional issues to include social, cultural, and economic concerns. Subfields of specialist academic interest have grown around spoiler groups in peace processes; truth recovery and attempts to deal with the past; and demobilization, disarmament, and reintegration (DDR). Other issues have received relatively scant attention: for example, the role of women and youth in peace processes; the long-term economic impact of peace initiatives; the relationship between peace and development; and indigenous approaches to peacemaking.

The Post-Accord Landscape

Until recently there has been very little analysis of post-settlement peacebuilding and the manifest difficulties facing post-accord states. Earlier research into the durability of peace settlements had reached pessimistic conclusions. Licklider's 1995 study of negotiated settlements between 1945 and 1993 found that only half of all negotiated settlements last beyond five years.[19] A 2001 study[20] suggested that most lasted for only three and a half years. The growing evidence of post-agreement instability has generated substantial new research attention. There is now a sufficient number of cases where peace accords either have been implemented, or have failed, to allow a broader audit of post-accord successes and failures.

Much of the research into post-agreement instability has taken place within disciplinary laagers:

- Political scientists have dominated the field, focusing on negotiations, postwar political instability, state failure, and new structures and institutions.[21] There is an impressive body of work on the peacekeeping role of the United Nations and other international bodies by international relations specialists such as Doyle, Johnstone and Orr.[22] Stedman and others emphasize the importance of external guarantors for peace agreements and the problems of spoilers.[23]

- Economists have identified the complexity of postwar economic reconstruction,[24] but have been insufficiently engaged with other social scientists for whom postwar reconstruction is also a major concern—a problem exacerbated by increasing evidence that postwar stability is closely associated with lack of postwar economic development.[25] The debate initiated by Collier, Hoeffler,[26] and colleagues at the World Bank, proposing that greed provides a better explanation than grievance for civil wars, has been strongly contested by many scholars, notably Arnson and Zartman.[27]

- Although scholars have recognized the need to engage the public sphere[28] in post-agreement peacebuilding, key constituencies, such as youth, have been neglected in the peace process literature. McEvoy-Levy's volume[29] is the first to examine the impact of youth on the legitimacy and sustainability of peace agreements. Kemper[30] has analyzed the roles of international organizations working with youth in war-to-peace transitions. This is a literature that is sure to grow given the increasing concern about the effect that "youth bulges" can have on social instability[31] and the interest of UNESCO, the World Bank, and others in post-conflict education. One continuing challenge is to better integrate the substantial literature on child soldiers,[32] the country-specific case studies and ethnographies of youth by psychologists and anthropologists,[33] and the political science and conflict studies literature on peace processes. Another is to balance the prevailing emphasis on children and youth as agents of violence with an analysis of their peacebuilding roles.

- There has been a growing interest in the rise in violent crime during post-accord periods, as evidenced in South Africa, Guatemala and El Salvador,[34] but there is still a shortage of empirical evidence and case studies, especially by criminologists. There is a strong literature on security issues such as policing reform, decommissioning, and demilitarization, including discussion of policy options for dealing with violence.[35] But at least one distinctive perspective, that of military strategists, is still severely underrepresented in the general academic literature on postwar implementation. Moreover, until recently, the contributions of young people to the security dilemmas of peace processes have been neglected.[36]

- A new field of inquiry has arisen, known as transitional justice, which examines how countries emerging from violence deal with its legacy. The field is a multidisciplinary one, with scholars from such varied fields as human rights, law, political science, anthropology, and philosophy examining such subjects as the pros and cons of truth commissions versus criminal trials, the consequences of postwar trauma, the connections between violence during and post-conflict, and the gendered dimensions of violence.[37]

- A recent step forward in analyzing post-accord issues has been the collaborative Research Initiative on the Resolution of Ethnic Conflict (RIREC) at the Joan B. Kroc Institute for International Peace Studies at the University of Notre Dame, which has examined the problems and challenges that develop after a peace accord has been reached between conflicting parties, but before the agreement has been fully implemented. It has focused on post-accord peacebuilding and the difficult question of how to create a sustainable just peace after a period of protracted conflict. The project has identified and integrated the study of three key dimensions of the post-accord landscape: post-accord violence, the role of young people in violent conflict and peacebuilding, and truth telling and peacebuilding. The three-year project resulted in three edited volumes[38] that are the basis for this book.

Why Peace Agreements Fail

The causes and dynamics of post-accord failure are varied. The problems and challenges which emerge when political violence has ended are new, so there are few guidelines available for tackling them. Violence is likely to continue from dissidents both within the government and ex-militia groups. Political instability is to be expected, because signatures on an agreement cannot banish the suspicions that led to the war in the first place. Parties may wish to renegotiate provisions in an agreement which they find unpalatable or cannot sell to their supporters. The expected peace dividend, heavily presented as an inducement to halt the fighting, is often disappointing. The transition from war to a stable and lasting peace is difficult and often fails.

The question is: why do agreements fail? The hypotheses offered as explanations are numerous and growing. Peace agreements fail for different reasons in different places, and any prescription about policy approaches is closely related to the appropriate diagnosis. Among the most popular explanations are:

The process or the agreement was flawed

The agreement did not include all the fundamental issues in dispute, or all the key actors, thus extending the post-agreement discourse into a new contested agenda. This was the case, for example, in Israel/Palestine and Rwanda.[39]

Failure to carry supporters past the agreement

The agreement may be perceived by one side—or occasionally by both sides—to have conceded too much to their opponents. This often leads to demands for a revision of the agreement, usually resisted with vigor by the opposing parties. Unless carefully managed, a sense of grievance may switch from the previously disadvantaged party to those who believe the pendulum has swung too far, as among Unionists in Northern Ireland.[40] Thus the problem of asymmetry continues, but in reverse, continuing to destabilize political life.

Failure to implement the agreement

Peace agreements lay out a broad agenda for postwar implementation, not a final settlement. Indeed, the post-negotiations negotiations are frequently particularly bitter, as the post-Oslo disputes demonstrate.[41] In order to sell the agreement, leaders persuade their followers that they have "won" the negotiations. Disillusion is almost inevitable.

Economic failure

Promises that an agreement will transform the economy are often frustrated, in two quite different ways. The international community or private enterprise may not be prepared to provide sufficient economic support for what they regard as an unproven settlement, and the expected peace dividend may not materialize. Even if a peace dividend materializes, it may be perceived as being unfairly distributed, as it was in South Africa, suggesting that the peace settlement has not fundamentally improved the condition of the less well-off in society.[42]

Security unrest

A peace agreement may formally end a war, but it may not remove the infrastructure of weapons, violence, and crime in postwar society. Crime rates rose significantly in Guatemala, El Salvador, and South Africa as ex-soldiers and ex-militants applied the skills learned during war to more selfish ends. Many academics emphasize the importance of external security guarantees, from the United Nations, regional organizations, or neighboring states.[43] The failure to guarantee security in Israel/Palestine constantly undermined the Oslo accords, and decommissioning of paramilitary weapons had a similar effect in Northern Ireland. At another level, the violence of the war years still demands recognition, or punishment, or forgiveness. The evidence is strong that violence may continue to destabilize the new society years after the agreement.

Failure to deal with past violence

Memories of the war, and grievances associated with it, rarely fade away spontaneously. The resurgence of demands for dealing with conflicts that occurred decades ago, in places as varied as Spain, Argentina, and Cambodia, is testament to the fact that past atrocities may still be powerful years after a conflict ends.[44] Coming to terms with past human rights violations is increasingly deemed to be imperative for the consolidation of both peace agreements and democracy. However, the question of *how* to deal with the past continues to be actively debated, with scholars questioning the appropriateness of different types of mechanisms. Early in the study of transitional justice, scholars fiercely debated the question of trials versus non-trial approaches,[45] and the debate took on an almost binary quality with books with such titles as *Truth versus Justice*[46] and *State Crimes: Punishment or Pardon.*[47] At this point, however, scholars have turned towards identifying the contexts under which societies are best served by punishments and those which are more conducive to other approaches. Truth commissions are no longer seen as a second-best option, employed only when prosecutions are not feasible. It is fair to say that the either/or characterization of dealing with past violence has given way to a plus/and one, in which both types of mechanisms are seen as complementary rather than adversarial. The most recent type of mechanism, one which has been used in Sierra Leone and which is likely to be used in other places, is the hybrid court, on which both national and international prosecutors and judges serve. This newest addition to the transitional justice repertoire is bound to have its own set of pros and cons.[48]

Failure to inspire or pacify the next generation
A sustainable peace agreement not only must carry along the negotiators of the accord and their immediate supporters but must also gain legitimacy in the eyes of the next generation. In most postwar contexts youth (under twenty-four) are sizeable minorities of the population and in many—Iraq and Sierra Leone, for example—they are the majority. Some are ex-combatants with special needs. Others may be traumatized by violence and displacement. Still more may have no memories of war (and no war weariness) but instead be socialized by a contentious and protracted peace process, as in Northern Ireland. Invariably, youth are politically marginalized, and along with economic hardship, continued unrest, and memories of past atrocities, this lack of voice may convince them to reject the peace agreement as flawed, illegitimate or a "sell-out."[49]

It should be noted that the same diagnosis cannot apply to postwar reconstruction in all countries. Moreover, in some contexts, it may take several, or all of these explanations, to explain the dynamics of failure.

The Research Jigsaw
Post-agreement research activity resembles a partly constructed jigsaw puzzle. Different research teams have assembled material on parts of the puzzle, but without the help of the completed picture. Parts of the jigsaw are well filled, and suggest appropriate policy approaches. Some areas are neglected, because they are unfashionable or unappreciated. There is too little discussion of the priorities for researchers and practitioners in the post-agreement landscape. A more radical criticism is presented by a growing number of scholars, who point to the inherent flaws in the "liberal peace process." Richmond[50] argues that failure to define the objective of peace is at the heart of the problem. Mac Ginty[51] suggests that the current approach to peacemaking does not address fundamen-

tal societal divisions, and consequently that failure is almost inevitable. Whether they are right or not, this is the right time to reconsider the reasons for success and failure in the post-agreement landscape. There is now a sufficient number of postwar cases to allow sensible comparisons.

Above all, there is often an absence of collaboration between research teams, and between the tasks they are attacking. Jeong and others argue the need for a synergetic approach, combining "public security, democratic transition, social rehabilitation, and development."[52] In a similar spirit, the three books upon which this publication is based identified three parts of the puzzle—violence, truth telling, and youth—and set out to focus serious research attention on them. This volume synthesizes and analyzes the lessons learned from the RIREC project and from other recent literature. It traces the dilemmas and tensions in the areas of violence, truth, and youth. The following three chapters take each of these issues in turn and examine the challenges each presents for peacebuilding after peace accords.

CHAPTER 2
Violence and Reconstruction

Post-accord Violence, and Why It Is Important

Calculations vary about how many comprehensive peace agreements have been signed since 1989, but they all share one common factor. They have all experienced post-agreement violence, and many agreements have collapsed as a result of failing to deal with it successfully.

As the contributors to *Violence and Reconstruction*[1] have demonstrated, postwar violence—and the motives of those who continue to use it—change after an agreement has been signed. Some state actors prefer to turn a blind eye to violence from sympathetic militias rather than to be seen undermining their own agreement. Spoilers who wish to continue violence after their colleagues have entered negotiations are not a homogeneous group, but are driven by a range of different motives to undermine the agreement, to affect its terms, or to engage in criminal activities. The most awkward challenge in dealing with post-agreement violence faces ex-militants who participated in the negotiations. Their involvement in the postwar political structures, often in a power-sharing government, will inevitably implicate them in responding to those who seek to overthrow it by violence—an uncomfortable position, as those using violence are using a similar justification to that used previously by the ex-militants themselves. Public frustration and disillusion is likely to grow if the leaders who negotiated the agreement are unable or unwilling to deliver a settlement. The danger is a return to entrenched and uncompromising positions, similar to the growth in electoral support for Sinn Féin and the Democratic Unionist Party in the years following Northern Ireland's Good Friday Agreement. First-time voters and young people, in particular, have gravitated towards the extremes.[2]

What's Known? What's Not?

In the great majority of cases, the reason for post-agreement collapses is violence, although its forms and effects have varied greatly from place to place. Research has focused particularly on disruptive violence from militants and ex-militants. In 1997, Stephen Stedman identified the part played by spoilers—"leaders and parties who believe that peace emerging from negotiations threaten their power, worldview, and interests, and use violence to undermine attempts to achieve it"[3]—in disrupting peace processes, and later highlighted in particular the political, economic, and security vulnerability of many states emerging from civil wars.[4] Since then there has been a healthy debate about the part played by spoilers in disrupting peace processes, and the subject continues to attract considerable research attention.[5] An impressive literature is also emerging about dealing with past violence through truth telling, using mechanisms such as truth commissions and trials.[6]

There are still substantial gaps. The vexing issues of demobilization, disarmament, and reintegration (DDR), especially in Africa, are attracting serious discussion,[7] but there is still insufficient understanding of why some problems have had such varied outcomes internationally. Weapons decommissioning, for example, was perhaps the major obstacle to post-agreement settlement in Northern Ireland in the seven years following the Good Friday Agreement, yet "over 850,000 ex-combatants have been disarmed in eight sub-Saharan states: Ethiopia, Angola, Eritrea, Liberia, Mali, Mozambique, Namibia, and Uganda."[8] Important debates on postwar crime rates, and on how policing should be adapted to postwar settings, are providing insights for policy making,[9] but there is still a shortage of empirical evidence and case studies. Although DDR and postwar crime are rarely confined within national boundaries, effective guidelines on appropriate regional and international policy approaches are still lacking.

So research into post-accord reconstruction, and into the problems of violence that frustrate it, is uneven. The reasons for this mixed picture are varied. Partly it arises from the very nature of violence. Postwar reconstruction requires the resolution of a wide range of problems, many of them difficult but most of them perceived as discrete. They include economic recovery and justice, law and order, education reform and rebuilding, and new political institutions; indeed every aspect of a functioning and fair society. Violence, however, infects the entire postwar landscape. It affects each of these other issues fundamentally. Its ubiquitous nature frustrates the study of its effects and the evolution of policies to address it.

Violence and Peace Processes

All peace processes must battle against the threat of violence, but its effects are neither universal nor constant. They vary between different settings, and between different stages in each setting. Although a peace process often follows open warfare between a militarized state and a guerrilla opposition, the level of violence may intensify during the pre-negotiation phase as combatants try to optimize their negotiating positions. The negotiations themselves are often accompanied by the emergence of more extreme dissident groups. Negotiators also have to confront a new range of high-priority issues, including demands for the early release of prisoners, disarmament and demilitarization, and policing reform, as well as the reintegration of militants into society and consideration of their victims. Although these patterns generally apply, they are also heavily influenced by local conditions. A peace process is not a predictable sequence from violence to settlement.

It is not uncommon for a peace process to be overturned by violence even after combatants have signed an accord. A peace agreement may be threatened from a range of sources: from elements within the state's political or military apparatus; from militant spoiler groups; and from the postwar interaction between violence, crime, and the community. In addition, the transfer from violence to stability raises security-related issues that are unavoidable in postwar societies: demobilization, disarmament, reintegration of soldiers and militants into society, policing reform. The balance between the threats varies according to local circumstances, but violence in some form or other is likely to be a challenge for the reconstruction of all postwar societies.

Violence by the state
The achievement of a peace agreement removes the glue that had held together disparate elements within the government during negotiations. Implementation of an accord is an exasperating and lengthy process. Even politicians involved in the negotiations may be expecting its downfall, and some may be working to bring it down. Political and security interests within a government often have different priorities, and different views about the durability of an agreement. Kristine Höglund and I. William Zartman argue that three main elements associated with the state may be tempted to explore a conflict rather than a peace approach: "the military, militias and decision-makers discontented with the turn to a settlement track."[10] The boundaries between them are often blurred. State actors opposed to an agreement, for example, may work in association with militias, or benefit covertly from militia activities, as they did in Congo-Brazzaville, Haiti, Guatemala, and El Salvador.

Who is to police the behavior of state actors during peace processes, especially after agreements have been reached? International organizations and other states usually work on the assumption that the state and its agencies, however corrupt and partial, have the prime responsibility for the maintenance of law, order, and governance during peace processes. But the state is also a primary actor in the conflict. It controls the greatest number of armed personnel and most of the weaponry, as well as the official agencies responsible for information and propaganda. It may seek to control the media, as in Burma and Zimbabwe. Illegal use of force by the state is often covert, usually denied, and always difficult to prove. So how are abuses by the state and by state personnel and agencies to be discovered and countered?

If a government abuses its power by continuing to use illegal violence, the principal onus for monitoring state behavior may fall on agencies operating wholly or partially outside the state. Human rights NGOs and election monitoring has played an important role in peace processes in El Salvador, South Africa, and elsewhere, and one of the strongest guarantees against the abuse of state power is a vigilant international press.

Violence by militants
The declaration of a cease-fire by militants is rarely undisputed, and its continuation is contingent on achieving concrete rewards during subsequent negotiations, such as early prisoner releases and the dismantling of the state's security apparatus. These rewards are rarely immediate. Consequently, the pendulum may swing back towards the militants who opposed negotiations in the first place. Four principal militant and ex-militant groups are contained within the range of the pendulum, all of them potential spoilers:[11]

> Dealers—those who are prepared to negotiate;
> Zealots—those whose goal is to spoil the process by bringing it down by violence;
> Opportunists—violent groups which may be persuaded, under some circumstances, to end violence; and
> Mavericks—those whose violence is primarily motivated by personal rather than political objectives.

If peace processes are to withstand the different forms of violence undermining them, different policy approaches are required towards these different interests. The key actors in any peace process are the Dealers, whose decision to negotiate initiated the process and without whose involvement the process ends. The key policy objective, it follows, is to ensure that they remain in the process. Their involvement as fully engaged partners is essential for effective reconstruction. It is not always easy to distinguish between Opportunists and Zealots. Both are usually smaller and more extreme groups that have either been excluded, or have excluded themselves, from the process. The essential difference is that the Opportunists may ultimately be open to participating in the process, while the Zealots are dedicated to its failure. The dilemma then is how to keep the door open for Opportunists while isolating the Zealots. If this is accomplished, the process must find a way of dealing with any remaining Zealots, as well as with any Mavericks who also continue to use violence. One measure of success is the degree to which violence can be criminalized by dealing with it through the courts. This becomes more feasible if the Dealers feel strong enough to condemn it. Dealers never find this easy, as it allows Zealots to charge them with betrayal, and to present themselves as the true patriots. Timing is crucial. In Northern Ireland, the universal fury at the August 1998 Omagh bomb, which killed twenty-nine and injured more than two hundred, and the marginalization of the bombers allowed Sinn Féin to condemn a republican bomb for the first time. However, the strength of Hamas and the Islamic Zealots in Israel/Palestine prevented Arafat and his successors from issuing such an unqualified condemnation.

Violence in the Community

After the declaration of a ceasefire, confrontations between ethnic rivals or with the security forces often replace the discipline of war. In Northern Ireland, for example, the peace process saw a return to more direct violence between Catholics and Protestants, especially during the annual marching season, when Unionist demonstrations and Nationalist protests raise the political temperature. The level of conventional crime is also likely to rise, for a range of reasons. Policing is dominated by security concerns. Many hostile areas are not patrolled, leading to an underreporting of crime statistics. Paramilitary organizations claim, and often exercise, the right to police the areas under their control. If an agreement is reached, these conditions may be reversed. The sharp rise in crime in Guatemala following the 1996 peace accords was "often the work of members of the existing police force or the army," as well as unemployed ex-combatants.[12] The criminal aspects of paramilitary campaigns often transmute into crime syndicates, particularly involving drug smuggling and dealing. The security services, more geared to dealing with political than conventional crime during the war years, are often ill equipped to deal with them. Underlying all of this, people have become accustomed to routine violence. Public expectations of immediate economic and social improvements, raised during the period of negotiations, are often disappointed after the accord is signed.

Postwar developments in South Africa and Northern Ireland illustrate the point. During the war years, crime rates were low in both places, but rose after the fighting stopped.[13] Postwar homicide rates in South Africa were dramatically high, but surprisingly constant in the years following the 1994 settlement. So was the number of reported rapes. Robberies, on the other hand, having decreased in the immediate postwar years, rose by 95.4 percent between 1996 and 2003. In 2003 the Mbeki government responded to criticism of the high crime statistics by recruiting another 8,000 policemen and improving police salaries, and claimed an immediate improvement when the number of murders fell by 8 percent during 2004, and robberies by 5.9 percent.[14]

Graph 2.1

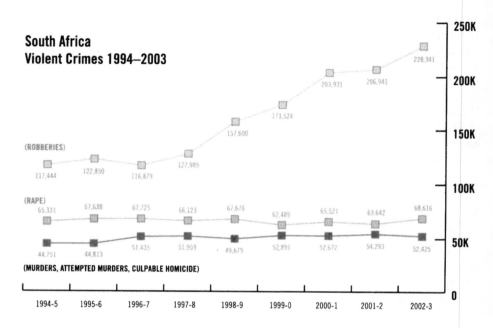

South Africa
Violent Crimes 1994–2003

(ROBBERIES)

117,444   122,850   116,879   127,985   157,600   173,524   203,931   206,941   228,941

(RAPE)
65,331   67,638   67,725   66,123   67,676   62,489   65,521   63,642   68,616

44,751   44,813   51,435   51,959   49,679   52,891   52,672   54,293   52,425
(MURDERS, ATTEMPTED MURDERS, CULPABLE HOMICIDE)

1994-5   1995-6   1996-7   1997-8   1998-9   1999-0   2000-1   2001-2   2002-3

Source: South African Police Service, *Crime Statistics*

The pattern was similar in Northern Ireland, albeit at a much lower per capita rate. The number of rapes was constant between 1995 and 2003, but the annual number of murders, attempted murders, and culpable homicides almost tripled during the period. Burglaries decreased, as they had in South Africa, by 19.8 percent between 1995 and 2000, and subsequently rose by 80.4 percent. Disguised among these statistics was a disturbing rise in punishment shootings and beatings, mainly by republican paramilitaries, and in organized crime and drug dealing by loyalists. In 2004 four people were killed by paramilitary organizations, the lowest total since the Troubles began in 1969. There were indications that republican paramilitary organizations had shifted their attention towards armed bank robberies, including the £22 million Ulster Bank robbery in 2004, attributed by the police and both the Irish and UK governments to the IRA (Irish Republican Army). Another alarming pattern change was an increase in attacks aimed at Northern Ireland's tiny but rapidly growing racial minorities. There were 212 reported racist incidents in the last eight months of 2003, 25 percent higher than the previous year.

In general, violent crime remained high in South Africa after the 1994 agreement, but shows some cautious signs of stabilizing. Violent crime appears to be rising in Northern Ireland eight years after the Good Friday Agreement, suggesting that post-accord countries should prepare for a similar increase.

Graph 2.2

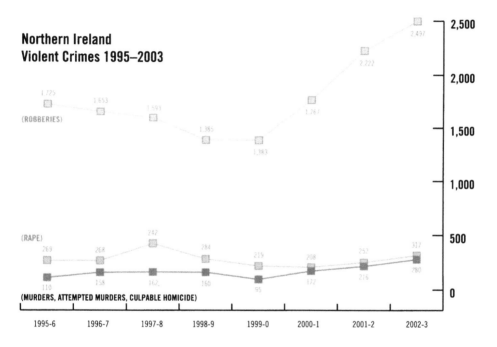

Northern Ireland
Violent Crimes 1995–2003

Source: Police Service of Northern Ireland, *Crime Statistics for Northern Ireland*

A significant rise in post-accord crime is clearly a matter for concern, but does it necessarily pose a threat to the agreement itself? Roger Mac Ginty's judgment is that crime has not been identified as the major factor contributing to the outright failure of a peace accord, but it can erode confidence in the agreement among the general population. As the sapping of Unionist support for the Good Friday Agreement in Northern Ireland demonstrates, the accord may survive, but be replaced only by an unstable and uncertain limbo. There are two more specific dangers: first, an authoritarian reaction from a government to crime may undermine "the liberalizing intentions and provisions of a peace accord"; and second, there may be an increase in vigilantism, a postwar problem deserving greater attention.[15] In Guatemala, vigilantes were responsible for the killing of dozens of suspected criminals in the six months after the signing of the accords in December 1996, including more than twenty lynchings in 1997 alone.[16]

Demobilization, disarmament, and reintegration (DDR) and police reform
All peace processes give rise to issues that could not be tackled while the fighting continued. Among the most common are demobilization, disarmament, and reintegration, and reform of the police and the security forces. Even if a peace agreement is signed, it can only signify agreement to sketch out the general parameters of how some of these issues should be approached. But the fine details and implementation—what du Toit has called post-settlement settlements[17]—form the new agenda for dispute. They are among the main tasks of the post-accord years.

Virginia Gamba passed somber judgment on recent international approaches to DDR: "Key objectives of a peace process are to secure peace, ensure demobilization, ensure disarmament, and assist in post-conflict reintegration and development. If these objectives are not realized, peace cannot be consolidated. Since 1989 almost all cases of multinational peace-making and peace support operations have not fully realized the above-mentioned objectives."[18]

Many of the worst failures highlighted by Gamba were in Africa, so it is ironic that Africa may be providing a model for other continents and regions through the New Partnership for Africa's Development (NEPAD), a cross-national body aiming to facilitate collaboration on DDR between African states. In Gamba's words, "the key of success on the ownership formula that led to the signature in Lusaka was that NEPAD was not presented as a hard and fast plan but as a hard and fast idea."[19] Most of all, it provided a mechanism for coordination not only between different functions (demobilization, disarmament, and reintegration), but also between the neighboring countries in the region.

Police reform can be an equally difficult and contentious postwar issue. The two main options facing societies are the integration of ex-militants into a new force, and reform of existing policing structures. The integration of ex-militants into the security system removes potentially disruptive soldiers and weapons from the street, legitimizes irregular policing activities, and provides additional police when they are most needed to deal with increased transitional violence. It certainly eased the transition in South Africa, but led to increased confrontations in the Palestinian territories. Reform of policing structures also raises tensions. The police are likely to be "reluctant reformers," so change is unlikely to be achieved rapidly. As Dominic Murray remarked: "The emerging police force, therefore, will now be tackling criminals who in the past may have acted as protectors of, and were protected by, the communities of which they form part . . . . In addition, the steps necessary to restore some form of normality (searches, curfews, check points, etc.) are exactly those most likely to engender antagonism."[20]

Whether integration or reform is adopted, the changes must be accompanied by significant retraining and restructuring. Policing of a peace process requires that the force must be acceptable to the community at large, which often implies significant changes in its composition. Behind these changes, in Murray's words, is "the overarching concept of trust."[21]

Violence as Catalyst for Peace

Occasionally certain atrocities provoke universal condemnation and galvanize popular reaction against the perpetrators. Responses to the 1998 Omagh bomb provided a springboard for post-accord progress in Northern Ireland. Security cooperation between the British and Irish governments improved; Sinn Féin's Gerry Adams openly criticized the bombers "without any equivocation whatsoever"; the Unionist leader David Trimble uncharacteristically complimented the Irish Republic. Within four days of the bombing, the group responsible—the "Real" IRA—had declared a ceasefire. Other groups soon followed. Violence, or rather spoiler violence, had become temporarily unfashionable. The responses to Omagh were dramatic, but not unique, in peace processes. The murder of a young town councilor, Miguel Ángel Blanco, in the Basque Country in 1997, and the 1992 massacre at Boipatong in South Africa produced similar spontaneous demonstrations of outrage. Instead of destabilizing negotiations or an agreement, they became a stimulus for negotiation.

Three factors are critical in converting atrocities into catalysts for peace: courageous leadership, the cohesion of the groups in negotiation, and timing. If these factors are in place, atrocities enable public outrage to be harnessed, rather than simply vented. The likeliness of this happening partly depends on the symmetry of power between, and cohesion within, the main parties. A more precise understanding of how violence influences post-accord reconstruction informs creation of the right strategy and right incentives to "tip the balance toward cooperation in deeply rooted ethnic conflicts."[22]

A Policy Package

Violence is unavoidable during peace negotiations, but it varies significantly in intensity and extent between different peace processes. For example, issues of demobilization and demilitarization significantly stalled postwar reconstruction in Northern Ireland, but did not cause serious problems in South Africa. It is important to analyze the distinctions between different forms of post-accord violence, because each form requires different treatment. The best safeguards against state violence, for example, are external monitors—international and regional organizations, NGOs, and a strong, independent media reporting illegal actions to the outside world—a reality recognized by the attempts of some governments to prevent or control monitors' access to scenes of violence.

An awareness of the distinction between different forms of violence is even more necessary when dealing with militants, because different types of spoilers require different treatment. Policy should reflect these distinctions. It should aim to support those ex-militants who have entered negotiations, to leave the door open for other militants to enter the process under strict conditions, and to apply the rule of law to isolate and sanction the Zealots and Mavericks who continue to use violence. Indeed, a further reason for distinguishing carefully between different forms of violence is that the appropriate policy for some of these problems may actually exacerbate others. For example, the traditional approach to postwar crime—an increased police presence on the streets—may not only provide targets for Zealots, but also lead to confrontations between police and activists, especially youth, as has happened in the Basque Country, Israel/Palestine, and Northern Ireland.

Whether the effects of violence are positive or negative depends on the ability of peacemakers to develop appropriate strategies in response to it. The contributors to *Violence and Reconstruction* demonstrate that successful postwar reconstruction requires leaders to think differently about violence, and to adopt three levels of response: a strategic approach; an incentives-based approach; and a reciprocal approach.

A strategic approach

At each stage of a peace process, and for each set of actors, the use of violence is primarily a matter of calculation rather than spontaneity. "In making decisions about the potential use of violence," as Marie-Joëlle Zahar contends, "militants and ex-militants assess the costs and benefits of each course of action."[23] Consequently, the resumption of violence can have either a positive or negative effect on postwar reconstruction. Sharp rises in the intensity of violence "force those at the negotiation table to make critical choices—essentially whether to recoil and return to the fight, or hunker down, continue talking, and weather the political storm."[24]

Under what circumstances can this tension be utilized to drive peace negotiations forward? While the use of violence increases distrust and disillusionment among opponents and may drive them back to war, in different circumstances, as Höglund and Zartman point out, "it may also influence the opposing side's fears of continued conflict, making it more determined in its attempts to pursue peace. With this use, violence can directly accelerate negotiations and the implementation of a peace agreement. Indirectly, violence by the state and its allies can have a reverse effect by raising opposition to violence and influencing public opinion in favor of the peace process."[25]

Timothy Sisk concludes that the central need is the management and reduction of uncertainty during negotiations and after agreements have been reached. He suggests a number of strategic requirements to reduce the negative effects of violence. These include the need to activate and support the moderate, centrist core; the need to evaluate intra-party dynamics, especially the rela-tionships between elites and mid-level elites, to ensure that leaders can carry their own supporters; and the need to remind people of the consequences of a return to violence, which are easily forgotten. Zahar argues, in addition, that the spoiler debate needs to be reframed within a broader context, and "focus on the interplay between motivation and context."[26]

An incentives-based approach

Successful reconstruction requires a combination of sanctions and rewards. Stedman and others have emphasised the importance of external custodians to consolidate peace agreements, but the allied use of incentives has received less attention. Each form of violence, at each stage in each peace process, needs to be separately identified, analyzed, and treated appropriately in order to gain better understanding of the factors that persuade different actors to reject vio-lence. Sisk points out, for example, that "the cost-benefit calculations of further fighting may be markedly different for different parties depending on their level of devotion to the conflict."[27] Within countries, he explains: "the electoral sys-tem is a key incentive structure that affects the propensity for rejectionists to foment violence. If a rejectionist party believes it can win a few seats in the new parliament, rather than being completely excluded from the new system, this incentive may be enough to widen the base of the peace process and bring in those with the capacity to 'spoil.'"[28]

Among the most effective incentives are examples of successful implemen-tation in other places. The best models for effective reconstruction are often, but not always, regional. In Guatemala and El Salvador, for example, approach-es to policing reform borrowed heavily and often profitably from Latin American and Spanish models that might have less relevance in other regions. In Europe too, there was a symbiotic relationship between approaches to nego-tiations in Northern Ireland, the Basque Country, and Corsica.[29] As discussed earlier, Virginia Gamba has pointed to the potential of New Africa's Partnership for Development (NEPAD) to provide a framework and inspiration for region-al DDR in Africa, and raises the question of its application in other places.

Negotiators are often eager to adapt new approaches. The use of "sufficient consensus"[30] to deal with the problem of multiple negotiators in South Africa is now commonplace in peace processes. Northern Ireland's Mitchell Principles introduced a model for attracting militants into negotiations while addressing the concerns of constitutional politicians. A peace process requires only minor incentives to encourage a more systematic search for the most appropriate and promising models.

A reciprocal approach

In November 1998, shortly after Andres Pastrana became president of Colombia, he took an exceptionally innovative gamble by declaring a large swath of southern Colombia a demilitarized zone and handing control over to the most powerful militant organization, the Revolutionary Armed Forces of Colombia (FARC). No reciprocal concessions were required, not even a cease-fire. His aim was to persuade FARC of his good intentions and to encourage the guerillas into negotiations. The experiment in confidence building failed. "By all accounts except their own, the rebels have abused the spirit of the government's inducement by stockpiling weapons, recruiting and training new fighters, killing perceived enemies and protecting lucrative drug operations."[31] Despite this failure, Pastrana gambled again in April 2000 with the second largest militant group, the National Liberation Army (ELN). He agreed to pull troops and police out of a northern region the size of Switzerland, but this time only in return for a national peace convention and after a "general framework of understanding" had been reached. The result was a decline in Pastrana's popularity among his own supporters and the failure of his venture.

The lesson of the Pastrana peace initiative in Colombia is that confidence-building measures—early release of political prisoners, policing reform, DDR—may reassure ex-militants, but are also likely to create anxiety among one's supporters. Unilateral confidence-building gestures are unlikely to succeed. Consequently, concessions between government and militants on issues of deep mutual suspicion must be carefully choreographed. Peace settlements "are package proposals that resolve multiple issues simultaneously by linking them."[32] The package is often assembled towards the end of negotiations, after the components in the package have been negotiated separately, often by separate teams. Interim announcements about partial agreements run the risk of undermining a comprehensive settlement, by subjecting it to premature scrutiny while talks on other matters continue. However, there are strong arguments for deliberately linking together some of the separate issues in dispute. Linking allows for greater flexibility in negotiation. It encourages the view that peace agreements are trade-off packages, and thus builds public confidence. In particular, it demonstrates to one's supporters that sacrifices have been made by their opponents as well as themselves. Some issues have particularly strong potential for linkages: early prisoner release and its effect on victims; demobilization and disarmament; and differing approaches to policing reforms.

The early release of prisoners is characteristically one of the earliest demands from militants. Victims' grievances, articulated through such mechanisms as truth commissions, are usually addressed much later, during the implementation of peace accords. The release of prisoners can help to build confidence in those initially suspicious of a peace process, but it also reminds relatives and friends of the lost victims—police, soldiers, security staff, and, most of all, civilians. At its most emotive level this includes the problem of the disappeared, when family members are still ignorant of the whereabouts of the bodies of their loved ones. Early releases of prisoners are likely to be more tolerable if they are accompanied by recognition of and compensation for the harm done to the bereaved and the wounded. Good policy thus considers sequencing; the sensitive issue of victims' compensation should be addressed during negotiations rather than post-settlement, not only for reasons of equity, but because general outrage may turn public opinion against the peace process itself, as evidenced in Israel and Northern Ireland.

The reciprocation between disarmament of militants and demobilization of security forces is obvious. It is natural for combatants to want to test their opponents' sincerity before disarming themselves, which can bring a peace process to stalemate. Consequently, there is need to orchestrate reciprocal concessions on demilitarization and decommissioning during peace negotiations, and to do this very early in the proceedings. The same applies to reform of the police and army. Whether ex-militants are integrated into the police force or army, or the forces are reformed internally, early implementation is also likely to enhance the chances of successful policing and security reform.

Reciprocation requires concessions from both government and its opponents. The ending of a war leaves a residue of lawlessness that sits uneasily in the no-man's-land between political violence and crime. Militant organizations are often reluctant to abandon the power and policing functions they had previously exercised, and violence may continue in the form of punishment beatings and killings, criminal activities, and vigilante attacks on those suspected of crimes. During negotiations, what ought to be unacceptable is accepted as necessary to achieve the greater good of a peace agreement. Uneasy distinctions are made between political violence that breaks the ceasefire, and other forms of violence that do not. It is essential to build into the agreement the recognition that all forms of violence may seriously undermine postwar reconstruction and that continuing ambivalence towards violence will not be tolerated. If the discussion is deferred until implementation starts, the advantages of reciprocity may be lost.

As the next two chapters demonstrate, violence can have pervasive effects on transitional justice and youth. The transitional justice mechanisms that emerge in post-agreement settings seek to address past violence while violence is still prevalent. Youth, often forming the majority of the population in post-accord settings, are a key set of actors in terms of DDR and policing reform as well as in relation to crime and post-accord violence in the community.

CHAPTER 3

The State of the Truth about the State: Lessons, Trends, and Challenges in the Field of Truth Telling

Truth is not only the basic condition for overcoming the past
but also the basic condition for developing
a nonviolent perspective for the future.[1]

Memory is the ultimate form of justice. Truth is both
retribution and deterrence, and undermines the mental
foundation of future human rights abuses.[2]

As Chapter 1 demonstrates, the threat of violence is very real, not only during conflicts, but in post-conflict periods as well. The quotes above almost perfectly summarize two emerging principles in the field of post-conflict reconstruction—that if a society coming out of a period of violent conflict does not publicly deal with its legacy of violence, history is likely to repeat itself; and, moreover, the very act of uncovering the truth about the past can deter political violence in the future. These principles also form the core ideas of the field of transitional justice, defined as attempts by new governments in regimes that have recently undergone a transition from dictatorship to democracy, or from armed conflict to peace, to establish procedures for holding accountable those responsible for gross violations of human rights, whether members of the former regime or those opposed to it. The term transitional justice itself, along with the identification of a distinct scholarly and practical field, is relatively new, dating back to the early 1990s. However, the issues, ideas, and mechanisms generally considered to fall under the ambit of transitional justice are considerably older, arguably dating back to the Holocaust, but certainly to the transitions to democracy in Latin

America in the 1970s and 1980s, with the end of military dictatorships and authoritarian governments there.[3] In country after country during that period of transitions, victims and survivors of the former regimes began to increase their demands for information about atrocities that had occurred under dictatorships. They wanted the truth about those periods to be uncovered and formally acknowledged, and they wanted those responsible for the atrocities to be held accountable. The study of confronting past violence during transitions to democracy was given additional impetus by the ending of the Cold War. Suddenly, questions about justice in times of transition were being asked in a wide variety of contexts, including Eastern Europe and Southern Africa, whose transitions are themselves attributable in part to global geopolitical consequences of the ending of the Cold War. At this point, uncovering the truth about human rights violations committed under both authoritarian and totalitarian regimes was increasingly deemed to be imperative for the consolidation of democracy.[4]

Transitional Justice
While no overarching theories of transitional justice exist, an issue which is returned to below, scholars and practitioners in the field argue that its core principles are legally grounded, and they point to the field's foundation in international jurisprudence.[5] Specifically, they point to the 1988 judgment by the Inter-American Court of Human Rights (IACHR) in the Velásquez Rodríguez case, which concerned a Honduran university student who had been detained without warrant by security forces and tortured under interrogation for alleged political crimes. The police denied the detention, effectively causing him to be disappeared. In the Court's opinion, because "there existed in Honduras from 1981 to 1984 a systematic and selective practice of disappearances carried out with the assistance or tolerance of the government," and further that "in the period in which those acts occurred, the legal remedies available in Honduras were not appropriate or effective to guarantee his rights to life, liberty and personal integrity," the state was responsible for violating the rights guaranteed to Velásquez Rodríguez by the Inter-American Convention on Human Rights, to which Honduras was a party.[6] In its findings, the Court laid out what were to become the framework and core principles of transitional justice. Specifically, the IACHR argued that states have six fundamental human rights obligations. The first is the obligation to prevent human rights violations. The second is the obligation to investigate alleged human rights violations. Failing to do so, or turning a blind eye to such allegations, makes the state complicit in these violations. Third, the state is obligated to identify victims and perpetrators and to disclose to the victims and society as a whole all that can be reliably known about the circumstances of the crime. Fourth, the state is obligated to punish the perpetrators, which is generally understood to mean prosecutions, although other forms of sanctions are also possible. Fifth, the state is obliged to provide

reparations, both monetary and nonmonetary, to victims or their survivors. Finally, states are obligated to eliminate from the ranks of the security forces those agents who are known to have engaged in such crimes. Juan Méndez details how these principles, first articulated in this case, have been further developed in international law and adopted by the United Nations as the standard norms in peace negotiations.[7]

How then do these obligations—and the concomitant rights they guarantee to citizens—translate into the practice of transitional justice? In general, four mechanisms are employed by countries in their efforts to confront their legacies of past gross violations of human rights.[8] The first is criminal prosecutions. Such attempts have run the gamut from wholly domestic courts to wholly international ones, such as the International Criminal Tribunal for Rwanda (ICTR) and the International Criminal Tribunal for the Former Yugoslavia (ICTY). Other prosecutorial approaches have included hybrid national/international courts, such as the Special Court in Sierra Leone, the Special Panels in Timor-Leste, and the forthcoming Cambodian tribunal.[9] The now-permanent International Criminal Court (ICC) is the most recent development to cement the idea that states are obligated to punish violators of human rights abuses, and that if they cannot or will not do so, the international community is obligated to do so in their stead.

The second transitional justice approach has been to adopt some form of a truth-seeking mechanism. This nonjudicial approach has often taken the form of a truth commission, which can go by a variety of names, from the now-common "Truth and Reconciliation Commissions" (TRCs) of South Africa, Sierra Leone, and Peru, to Guatemala's "Commission on Historical Clarification." While no two commissions are the same, the term "truth commission" has come to refer generically to a particular type of transitional justice mechanism, created in a post-conflict situation to examine past atrocities, issue findings of responsibility, and make future-oriented recommendations designed to foster and consolidate democracy and a human rights culture.[10] Priscilla Hayner notes the common features of truth commissions: they are institutions officially sanctioned by the state; they have temporary mandates (generally ranging from six months to two years); they focus on investigating patterns of abuse that occurred over a particular time period (as opposed to an inquiry into a specific event); they almost always focus on politically motivated repression; they are nonjudicial (i.e., they do not have the power to prosecute); they are created during periods of political change to foster the transition to democracy; and they issue final reports that contain recommendations for future actions by the state to ensure that the transition is sustainable.[11] Over thirty commissions have existed in the past, have very recently completed their work, are currently in operation, or are slated to begin operations in the near future.[12] While truth commissions are perhaps the most well-known truth-telling mechanism, other forums for uncovering the truth of past violence also exist, including commissions of inquiry and investigations by national human rights commissions.

The third approach for delivering transitional justice is reparations. While monetary reparations are usually foremost in people's minds, other forms of reparations are also deemed important for repairing past harms and restoring lost rights. These include symbolic forms of reparation such as monuments and museums, the issuing of official apologies, the restitution of stolen properties, or the granting of privileged access to public services such as health care.

The fourth transitional justice approach is institutional reform. One of the core ideas of transitional justice is that of *Nunca Más* (Never Again)—that a primary goal of undertaking a transitional justice exercise is to prevent future human rights violations. One way to do so is by reforming those institutions which abetted the collapse of the rule of law and the accompanying rise in human rights violations. Those institutions targeted for reform typically include the judicial system, the police force, and the military. Other institutions might also be included, such as the media. One reform that relates to the final obligation articulated by the IACHR case noted above, the obligation to remove perpetrators from positions of authority, is vetting—the process of removing abusive, corrupt, or incompetent public employees in an effort to build more effective and trustworthy institutions.[13]

Space constraints do not allow for an in-depth analysis of all four mechanisms; thus, for the purposes of providing an overview of the trends and lessons learned, as well as the challenges and limitations in the field, this chapter will concentrate primarily on truth seeking as a transitional justice mechanism, as did all of the authors contributing to the RIREC volume *Telling the Truths: Truth Telling and Peace Building in Post-Conflict Societies*.[14] In many ways, the three other mechanisms (prosecutions, reparations, and institutional reform) can be subsumed under truth-seeking exercises. Both trials and truth commissions are, of course, public, officially sanctioned institutions for uncovering the truth, and states are not restricted to one type of truth-telling mechanism—indeed, states are increasingly experimenting with multiple truth-telling mechanisms either sequentially or simultaneously. Moreover, almost all truth commissions are mandated to make recommendations to the state and civil society. Almost invariably they include recommendations on reparations and institutional reform. The Moroccan truth commission was in fact tasked with distributing reparations. The South African commission included a twenty-five-page chapter on reparations in its final report, along with a forty-five-page chapter on other recommendations, many of which were geared towards institutional reform.

In sum, the idea that truth telling is a necessary—albeit never sufficient—ingredient in peacebuilding has become an accepted norm in the fields of peace studies and conflict resolution.[15] Several scholars have noted the ever-increasing acceptance of this norm. David Mendeloff notes that a "general consensus has emerged" on the need for states and societies to come to terms with their past, noting that "scholars and practitioners of peacebuilding, as well as publics of war-torn societies, increasingly agree that some kind of formal accounting of the past is essential to achieve lasting, 'self-enforcing' peace in war-torn societies." As a result, Mendeloff observes, formal truth-telling mechanisms have become "part of the standard repertoire" of international peacebuilding activities.[16] Similarly, Rosalind Shaw notes that truth-telling mechanisms, such as truth commissions, are regarded as "a standard part of conflict resolution 'first aid kits.'"[17] Enough data now exist across a number of cases to allow for an exploration of lessons learned along with the challenges which remain in the field of truth telling.

Lessons Learned and Trends in the Field
What follows is an overview of several key lessons learned through the knowledge accumulated in several dozen truth-telling exercises. This is by no means an exhaustive list, and many other lessons and trends could be added. The first three issues can be read primarily as lessons learned, while the final three are more appropriately viewed as trends in the field.

Transitional justice should be context specific
There is no single "correct" approach to transitional justice, and practices from one setting are not always appropriate for another. Each context is unique and will demand unique solutions. Applying this lesson to truth telling, anthropologist Rosalind Shaw has drawn particular attention to (and is critical of) the fact that a very specific type of truth telling—the public recounting of memories—has become the standard practice. She is critical as well of the assumption underlying this practice: that the public revealing of these memories will lead to a sense of healing for victims. This assumption, and its associated practice of public hearings for victims, was epitomized by a popular slogan used by the South African TRC: "Revealing is Healing." Based on her work in Sierra Leone, Shaw rejects this notion, arguing that the conciliatory and therapeutic efficacy of truth telling is "the product of a Western culture of memory deriving from North American and European historical processes."[18] As such, Shaw rejects as problematic the assumption that verbally remembering violence is universally beneficial. In Sierra Leone, for example, social forgetting—as opposed to public verbalizing—constitutes the cornerstone of reconciliation and reintegration. Speaking of the violence, especially in public, is viewed as encouraging its return, calling it forth when it is just beneath the surface and might at any moment re-erupt. The mention of violence would undo a "cool heart," which is a ritual designed to reverse the work of combatants who turned children into soldiers and restore the child's relationship with its ancestors and God through small offerings and consecrated water. Because having and maintaining a "cool heart" requires a transformation of social identity, ex-combatants are urged not to talk publicly about the war after these rituals and community members are

discouraged from referring to ex-combatants as "rebels" or other labels. Both sides are told not to speak of or ask about the past actions of the person and not to discuss the war in public. In this way, past violence is "unmade" and new social persons are "made." Community reconciliation results in this case not through talking but precisely from silence. For Shaw, then, the fact that in her analysis the international community "pushed" public hearings on victims and survivors through a truth commission may well have undermined the peace-building process. The policy implication of the recognition that healing, recon-ciliation, and justice are culturally specific is clear: survivors themselves should identify the problems they believe obstruct their ability to heal, as well as deter-mine the interventions necessary to overcome them.

Studying best practices can avoid past mistakes
At the same time that scholars and practitioners need to ensure that transition-al justice mechanisms are culturally appropriate, they should also study past experiments with truth telling, to learn and adopt the best practices to date, as well as to avoid some past pitfalls. A case in point is the absence of inclusion of gender in the mandate of the South African TRC. As noted in more detail below, the TRC—partly as a result of its mandate—was not terribly successful at uncovering the truth about gender-specific gross violations of human rights, including rape and other forms of sexual violence. An interesting hypothesis to examine would be whether a connection can be found between the TRC's fail-ure to adequately address gender-based violence during apartheid and the high rates of gender-based violence, including rape and domestic violence, in post-apartheid South Africa. In contrast, the enabling act of the Sierra Leone Truth and Reconciliation Commission (SLTRC) made explicit reference to gender-based violations and specifically mentioned women as a special target group, mandating the commission to pay special attention to the "subject of sexual abuses and to the experiences of children within armed conflict."[19] Moreover, in contrast to South Africa, the SLTRC was mandated to record "violations and abuses of human rights and international humanitarian law related to armed conflict." Interestingly, the SLTRC was a mixed commission with both national and foreign commissioners, one of whom was Yasmin Sooka, a former South African commissioner, who was able to help the Sierra Leonean commissioners apply the lessons learned from the South African case. Sooka argues that when the three mandates (focusing on gender-based violations, sexual abuses, and war crimes) were read together, the SLTRC was able to apply a much wider, more comprehensive definition of gross violations of human rights there, one which specifically included gender-based violations. As a result, Sooka concludes, unlike in South Africa, women and girls came out in large numbers to speak to the Sierra Leone commission.[20]

Other important corrections of past mistakes can be gleaned from the Panamanian and Peruvian truth commissions. In Panama, whose commission released its final report in 2002, a Follow-Up Office for the Objectives of the Truth Commission was created, thus attempting to overcome the widespread problem of no government or civil-society agency being tasked with taking up the work of a truth commission once it ceased to exist. In South Africa, for example, no organization was assigned the tasks of disseminating the report or of ensuring that its recommendations were implemented. Méndez observes that Panama's follow-up office "is an important contribution to the development of individualized truths and to dealing objectively and seriously with repara-tions."[21] Finally, the Peruvian TRC, which issued its report in 2003, attempted to bridge the gap between truth telling and the formal seeking of justice, a gap which often serves to foster the criticism that societies that adopt truth com-missions eschew justice for victims and their survivors. To correct this, the Peruvian TRC established a special unit in charge of recommending cases for prosecution. Méndez concludes that not only is "the development of a very explicit relationship between truth and justice the most significant contribution made by the Peruvian TRC," but that "the Peruvian TRC will be the new para-digm in truth commissions."[22]

The field of transitional justice is thus not static; it is ever evolving and prac-titioners are learning to walk that fine line between being context specific while at the same time borrowing best practices from other settings.

The international community's interest is fleeting, if it is present at all
Mark Freeman argues that transitional governments must take advantage of the small window of opportunity at the moment of transition when the internation-al community is likely to show an interest in assisting and funding transitional justice mechanisms before shifting their attention to the next "hot spot."[23] Sometimes, this fleeting interest means that the international community is at odds with local needs, as mechanisms such as prosecutions and truth commis-sions are often more likely to succeed when they are implemented gradually, only after additional stability has been achieved. Geopolitics and lack of strate-gic importance are part of the interest/non-interest mix as well. Charles Taylor, former Liberian head of state and the person considered the principal architect of the civil war there as well as a primary instigator in the 1990s of wars throughout West Africa, including Sierra Leone, is a case in point. His arrest and prosecution was consistently deemed a high expectation of the Special Court for Sierra Leone (SCSL) by Sierra Leoneans, especially after his indictment in 2003 on seventeen counts of crimes against humanity. Taylor fled to Nigeria from Liberia in the same year; under a deal brokered primarily by the Nigerian and U.S. governments, he agreed to go into exile and stay out of politics. This deal ended with his arrest in March 2006, and his extradition to Sierra Leone, and eventually to The Hague to stand trial. Despite repeated violations of the terms of the agreement (it was speculated that he continued to manipulate Liberian politics from exile), the international community was long unwilling

to pressure the Nigerian government to deliver Taylor to the Special Court. Nigeria did so only after it could no longer justify his asylum in the face of his requested extradition by a democratically elected government in Liberia whose request was supported by the United States.

In addition to lack of interest, political realism, which manifests itself as lack of pressure in the best-case scenario, and outright obstructionism in the worst-case, is evident around the world. The refusal of Indonesia to extradite suspects to Timor-Leste stands alongside the fact that Radovan Karadzic, former Serbian Republic president, and his former general, Ratko Mladic, have not yet been arrested for war crimes and genocide a full decade after their indictments by the ICTY. Moreover, their eventual arrest, should it happen, is likely to be more related to the international politics of European integration than the justice needs of victims.

Perhaps the biggest problem, however, is the apathy of the international community. While a lack of sustained support in terms of money and time are problems, they occur in countries which have at least captured the attention of the international community. Far worse off are the countries that have not even made it onto the international radar screen, or about which the international community appears to simply not care. David Crane, special prosecutor to the SCSL, notes this challenge in relation to Africa: "All too often, in places where the light of the law never shines—the dark corners—a horror erupts that shocks the international community. This condition is spawned by indifference bred by lack of understanding for or care about the region concerned . . . . West Africa simply is not important to a jaded world suffering through the agony of a confused and uncertain future in Iraq. This focus has completely put West Africa back into its dark corner, war crimes tribunal and all."[24]

Hybrid tribunals are the wave of the future, which could be a problem

The ICTY and ICTR are wholly international, established, funded, and overseen by the United Nations, which appoints prosecutors and judges. In contrast, the newest form of transitional criminal prosecution is the hybrid court: criminal tribunals—such as those in Sierra Leone and Timor Leste, and the soon-to-be-inaugurated Cambodian court—with both national and international prosecutors and judges. The potential problem of clashing national and international goals noted above is evident in the very reason why these courts have become so popular. The idea behind hybrid courts is that they will rectify perceived flaws of the ad hoc tribunals for Yugoslavia and Rwanda, which are seen as dragging on for far too long and at too great an expense-highlighted by Slobodan Milosovic's trial having dragged into its fifth year, only to have Milosovic die before any verdicts were rendered, denying his victims both criminal justice and closure.

To this end, the SCSL, an early hybrid court, faced immediate pressure from the international community to conduct its work quickly and efficiently.

The Court was expected to operate for three years on a budget less than $60 million, and to try only a handful of cases.[25] The new hybrid approach to prosecutions was touted as the next generation of international criminal justice institutions, operating in-country and thus keeping costs low. Beth Dougherty argues that the SCSL faced an "enormous burden of proving that the hybrid model could make international criminal justice effective, efficient and inexpensive."[26] She is critical of the international community for this, calling its expectations "unrealistic" and pointing out that a three-year window of operation, even if the court indicted only the expected fifteen to twenty individuals, was too narrow, especially as the court had to begin its work from scratch, including having to build physical spaces to both hold and try criminals.

The international community then further undermined the likelihood that the Court could ever meet its expectations by dragging its feet in providing funding for it. While Kofi Annan's initial report to the Security Council on the establishment of the SCSL called for the court to be funded through member assessments, as the ICTY and ICTR are, the council countered with a proposal to fund the court through voluntary contributions. While Annan repeatedly warned that with such funding the court would be neither viable nor sustainable, the council insisted on its proposal. Despite Annan's slashing of the original $115 million budget for three years of operation, at which the Council balked, to $57 million in June 2001, by December of that year only $14.8 million had been received for the first year of operation, with only $20.4 million pledged for the next two years. This left a $21 million shortfall. In its second year of operation, of the $20.4 million pledged, only $14 million was received. This resulted in yet more severe cutbacks, with the insistence that $10 million be cut from the $30 million budget for the third year of operation, which was already 30 percent lower than the SCSL request.[27] Current estimates are that the final cost of the court will be less than the ICTY spends in a single year. [28]

In other words, the international community's growing concern with "UN bloat" led it to demand efficiency, in terms of both time and money, rather than focusing on what was required in the context of Sierra Leone, which was emerging from a decade of brutal civil war and deemed by the United Nations to be the world's poorest country. Having insisted that the Court complete its operations in three years, the international community then set about ensuring that it could never achieve this. There are thus serious consequences to the emerging trend to hybridize international justice, including a sometimes unsettled relationship between the courts—set up by the United Nations on behalf of the international community—and the local populations they are meant to serve. The international community must find the right balance between too much involvement in transitional justice on a national level, in terms of insisting on certain criteria to fill demands unrelated to local needs, and too little involvement, through failure to fund transitional justice projects or failure to support them for however long it takes.

Trials and truth commissions are not either/or propositions
Early approaches to transitional justice viewed truth telling in an "either/or" manner—states either had the means to prosecute perpetrators, or they did not. In the latter cases, the best that new governments could hope for was a truth commission. In this early iteration, truth commissions were seen as a second-best option for societies transitioning to democracy, employed when prosecutions were not feasible because of amnesties, the threat of violence, or lack of judicial resources. In this view, summed up as the "truth versus justice" dilemma, trials were assumed to always be preferable to any non-trial truth telling. However, as the international criminal courts for Yugoslavia and Rwanda—considered the pinnacles of international justice—dragged on and became bogged down, it soon became clear that only a very small fraction of perpetrators would ever be indicted, and as the benefits of truth commissions became more evident, this either/or characterization has been supplanted by a "plus/and" one.

In other words, most conflict resolution experts, transitional justice scholars, and human rights activists now view the two types of mechanisms as complementary rather than adversarial. Each has its benefits and drawbacks, and states need to figure out how to capitalize on the strengths of each. For example, as Bronwyn Leebaw points out, whereas trials focus on very specific events from the past, truth commissions tend to paint a larger picture, investigating historical eras that claimed thousands of victims. Likewise, whereas trials are capable of trying only a small number of perpetrators, truth commissions can fill in knowledge gaps by explaining broad underlying causes of violence. Moreover, whereas trials hear testimony of a relatively few victims and witnesses, truth commissions can provide forums for many victims to tell their stories; the likelihood that the average citizen will ever appear before a tribunal is remote. This is especially true when special transitional justice tribunals are established with mandates limited to investigating only the most atrocious and heinous crimes and only the architects of those crimes.[29] As Alex Boraine, former president of the International Center for Transitional Justice (ICTJ), points out: "a Special Court will try 15 people but what about the 16th and the 18th person?"[30]

Transitional justice may also be found in non-transitional settings
An interesting recent trend is the examination of historical atrocities during non-transitional moments. Two cases highlight this trend. The first is the Greensboro Truth and Reconciliation Commission (GTRC) in North Carolina. Established in June 2004, the commission is investigating the events surrounding the shooting deaths of five protestors and the wounding of ten others by the Ku Klux Klan and the American Nazi Party on November 2, 1979. While adopting the methodologies of other commissions, such as statement taking and public hearings, in many ways the GTRC represents a departure from what is traditionally thought of as a truth commission, by investigating a single incident

as opposed to a pattern of abuses, as well as the fact that it was not created during a period of political change to foster the transition to democracy. Indeed, because it was established by a coalition of civil society groups with municipal government support, Louis Bickford of the ICTJ refers to the GTRC as an "unofficial truth project."[31] Still, it has been self-consciously modeled on truth commissions elsewhere, as noted on the commission's Web site: "The Greensboro Truth and Reconciliation Commission is based upon similar efforts around the world, most notably in South Africa. Building on this wealth of international experience, Greensboro represents the first application of this model in the United States."[32]

The second case involves Morocco, where in April 2004, King Mohammad VI inaugurated the first truth commission in the Middle East, the Equity and Reconciliation Commission (IER), which submitted its final report to the king on November 30, 2005. The Commission was mandated to establish the truth about serious human rights violations that occurred between 1956, when Morocco became independent, and 1999, when Mohammad VI assumed the throne, including the identification of institutional (but not individual) responsibilities, providing reparations to victims, and issuing recommendations for reforms to prevent the recurrence of violations.[33] While the IER emerged from a transition, it was a monarchical transition (from the late King Hassan II to his son Mohammad VI), rather than a transition from war to peace or from authoritarianism to democracy, the contexts in which truth commissions generally are established.

It remains to be seen whether the lessons learned from transitional justice experiments conducted in transitional contexts apply to nontransitional settings. Moreover, applying these methods to new contexts is likely to bring new challenges. Nowhere is this more evident than in debates surrounding the feasibility of applying transitional justice methods when there are no longer any living perpetrators or victims. Questions surrounding the granting of reparations for slavery in the United States—including who can stand in the place of victims in terms of remedy, whether one needs to prove a linked disadvantage in order to validate a claim, and how to calculate claims—are indicative of the difficult challenges of applying transitional justice approaches to long-term legacies of abuse—those in which the grievances of the dead lie beyond even the memories of the living.

Challenges and Limitations of the Field

While lessons and best practices continue to accumulate, there is much that remains unknown about what works and does not work in terms of transitional justice. Like the list of lessons and trends above, what is offered here are only a few insights into the challenges and limitations of the field; many others could be added.

Methodological weaknesses
At this point, the field is stronger theoretically than empirically, with little hard data on what works where and why. One reason for this may be a number of significant methodological issues, including lack of agreement about how to evaluate the success of transitional justice exercises. Indeed, the primary focus of several of the contributors to *Telling the Truths: Truth Telling and Peace Building in Post-Conflict Societies* was addressing these methodological weaknesses.

At its most basic, there is little agreement on what "success" would look like. Timothy Garton Ash highlights just how difficult assessing the success of a truth commission can be by asking, "by what criterion is 'success' to be judged, in the first place? Is it Truth? Justice? Reconciliation? Closure? Healing? National Unity? Prevention of future abuses?"[34] Even if this question were settled among scholars and practitioners-which it is not-the "success" question would still be fraught. How would one go about determining the level of reconciliation, or the degree of healing, or how much national unity has been achieved, or how much national unity is "enough" to declare a truth-telling exercise successful?

A second issue is that of time. How long after the conclusion of a truth commission must one wait before confidently assessing its impact—or how soon can one proceed? It may, of course, take decades to achieve some of the goals of truth telling, such as healing or reconciliation. Moreover, for peace to be deemed truly sustainable, it cannot apply only to the current generation, or even the next one; it must be multigenerational. Indeed, when the violations have been so terrible, reconciliation is sometimes possible only between the children or even the grandchildren of survivors, as Dan Bar-On has noted in relation to the Holocaust.[35] Another time-related issue is the lack of longitudinal data to study impacts over time. Victoria Baxter notes that data that measure attitude changes of a particular cohort over time are nearly nonexistent, partly because it can be difficult to stay in touch with victims over time. This problem is compounded by the lack of baseline data showing attitudes towards reconciliation before truth telling was initiated.[36] These time-related issues can pose a challenge for studying the long-term impact of a truth-telling mechanism.

A third assessment issue involves isolating the effects of a particular truth-telling experience. The establishment of a truth commission never occurs in a vacuum; it is always part of much broader societal change, in which improvements in such areas as democracy and human rights may already be underway, initiated by post-transition governments that have been put in place prior to the establishment of any commission. It is not always clear, for example, whether particular effects—such as enhanced trust in the judiciary—can be attributed to the work of a truth commission or to other dynamics of the transition period.

As a result, Eric Brahm notes: "there are antecedent conditions that cloud one's ability to distinguish what independent effect a truth commission has had on a society in transition."[37] In fact, these prior conditions may well need to be in place in order for truth telling to be effective. Moreover, Mendeloff points to the difficulty of determining the direction of the causal arrow, arguing that the hypothesis that peace creates the conditions for truth telling to take place is just as plausible as the reverse hypothesis—that truth contributes to peace.[38]

Finally, the multidisciplinarity of the field of transitional justice is both one of its strengths and one of its weaknesses. From a methodological standpoint, the fact that concepts such as reconciliation, truth, and justice are interpreted differently by theologians, political scientists, psychologists, philosophers, and lawyers can add to a lack of conceptual clarity, a general problem plaguing the study of transitional justice.[39] Baxter attributes conceptual confusion in part to the lack of a generalized transitional justice theory to anchor a consistent and common understanding of key concepts.[40]

Gender is frequently inadequately incorporated

In the more than thirty truth commissions which have existed to date, none has been chaired by a woman. Even more significant has been the systematic under-reporting by women of violations that they personally suffered, as opposed to those suffered by their fathers, husbands, and sons, about which women have been more willing to testify. While the endemic use of rape as a tool of war is now well-known,[41] one would be hard-pressed to find evidence of this in women's testimony before truth-telling mechanisms. In South Africa, for example, over 21,000 victims' statements were taken; only 140 explicitly mentioned rape.[42] Women in general find it difficult to discuss their experiences of rape and other forms of sexual violence—this is true in private, and even more so in public forums like commission hearings. There are undoubtedly many reasons why this is the case, some of which are generalizable across cultures, others of which are context specific.

In the South African case, some women chose not to testify out of a sense of shame. Others refused to talk out of fear that they would be rejected by family members who had no prior knowledge of the abuse. Still others felt that bringing up old memories of sexual assault was too painful, certainly in terms of answering questions about it in a public forum. Some felt that they simply did not have the language to express what they had endured. Some women were aware that their rapes were symbolic acts meant to humiliate men for not being able to protect them and for that reason felt that testifying would only further humiliate men.[43] Some women feared that they would no longer be marriageable, while others feared retaliation. Some women, according to Fiona Ross, were loath to make statements that their children might one day read.[44]

The lack of truth telling about the magnitude of gender-based violence was exacerbated by the fact that no man applied for amnesty for the crime of rape or for any other sexual violation. The reasons for this are not clear, but one can surmise several explanations. One is that any potential amnesty applicant likely knew that proving the presence of required criteria (political motivation, proportionality, and absence of malice) would be extremely difficult. Another is that raping women was simply not deemed a serious enough crime to warrant opening oneself up to public exposure and censure. Finally, some potential applicants may have wagered on the likelihood that few women would publicly testify about their rapes and would likely not be willing to name names, for all of the reasons already noted. Thus, only 140 women testified about rape before the commission, and no men admitted to it. One could surmise from this that rape was not a serious problem for South African women; in doing so, one would be wrong. Rather, what existed in South Africa was a profound silence about women's experiences of violence during apartheid; neither victims nor perpetrators were willing to reveal the truth about these experiences. Former TRC Commissioner Yasmin Sooka has referred to a "conspiracy of silence" between victims and perpetrators.[45]

Whatever the reasons for underreporting by both women and men, it hinders a truth commission's ability to uncover the full truth about past atrocities. And, if the core principle of transitional justice—that is, that failure to deal with the past is likely to contribute to continued violations in the future—holds, then one should be concerned about a truth-telling mechanism's ability to contribute to a fully human rights-respecting culture, one which respects both gender justice and gender equity.

Political rights are prioritized over economic rights
Most truth commissions are mandated to examine politically motivated crimes. In general, this means that they focus on specific civil and political rights. In the South African case, the TRC was mandated to examine only what are known as bodily integrity rights, which included those rights enshrined in the South African constitution and under international law, including the right to life, the right to be free from torture, the right to be free from cruel, inhuman, or degrading treatment or punishment, and the right to freedom and security of person, including freedom from abduction and arbitrary and prolonged detention."[46] The reality, of course, is that many victims of gross violations of civil and political rights have also suffered violations of social and economic rights. Especially when victims formed part of a targeted minority, access to education and jobs may have been denied, and property of all kinds (including livestock) may have been destroyed. As a result, many people not only are forced to deal with the aftermath of personal suffering from violence, but must also deal with the realities of extreme and crushing poverty. These issues, however, generally do not fall under the ambit of truth commission investigation. This reality sometimes has severe consequences, such as the fact that in South Africa victims of forced removals, Bantu education, or any other of a myriad of laws

passed by the apartheid government, or of the effects of those laws, including hunger, poverty, and the lack of basic health care, would not be deemed victims by the TRC, and thus ineligible for reparations. The focus on civil and political rights to the exclusion of social and economic rights also has gendered consequences since women, as the most vulnerable group in society, are more likely than men to suffer the effects of structural violence. Ross argues that the consequences for South African women are profound: "Permitting the expression of pain of a particular kind, [the commission] emphasized bodily violation at the expense of a broader understanding of apartheid and its consequences. Foregrounding certain forms of violence in the public record, it rendered some kinds of pain more visible while displacing other forms of experience and its expression."[47]

It is not clear that truth-telling mechanisms are the best venue for examining violations of economic rights. With their relatively short time frames and the undoubtedly large increase in number of potential victims who would fall under their purview, charging these mechanisms with examining the causes and consequences of poverty, and with establishing individual guilt for economic crimes, may well decrease their ability to accomplish their work in any sort of effective way. On the other hand, there is no doubt that a nexus exists between violations of civil and political rights, and social and economic rights. To date, examinations of the former have taken precedence over the latter.

What happens to recommendations?
Almost all existing research on truth commissions is retrospective in nature, looking backwards at particular aspects of their work, such as whether they fulfilled their own stated goals and how much truth was revealed. In contrast, almost no research examines what states have done with the information handed to them by commissions, including the status of recommendation implementation and why some recommendations are implemented and others are not. Rather than making a commission itself the site of inquiry, it may be more fruitful to turn the focus onto the state if we are interested in understanding truth commissions' long-term impact on societies. Brahm refers to this as the distinction between the measure of a commission's "success" (i.e., the degree to which a commission fulfilled its assigned duties) as opposed to its "impact" (i.e., the broader purposes to which a commission's work is put). He notes that it is one thing to uncover the fact that the judiciary and police forces were involved in atrocities (an example of a success); it is quite another to determine that a truth commission has contributed to their institutional reform (an example of an impact).[48] In terms of enhancing human rights and the rule of law, these commissions cannot create reconciliation or bring peace by themselves, despite the fact that they are often described as if they can do both.

If one wishes to gauge the long-term impact of truth commissions, the focus needs to turn to what happens after commission truth telling—in particular, what happens to the reports produced by truth commissions and to the recommendations they contain. In other words, although truth commissions are mandated to look to the past, the study of their long-term contributions must necessarily be future oriented and include examining what happens with the recommendations and the reports they produce. If recommendations and reports are quickly forgotten once the commission has formally ended, and if the state refuses to implement and monitor the recommendations made to it to effect these changes, it seems unfair to hold the commission accountable for failing to foster a human rights culture or the rule of law—especially given that the commission is not given the power to compel governments to act on its recommendations. Moreover, most commissions shut down and disappear long before most recommendations can be tackled. And yet, many of the claims made about the long-term benefits of truth commissions hinge on whether recommendations are implemented; this is especially true in terms of human rights and the rule of law, since many commission reports focus on institutional failures, in particular in the judicial system, police force, and the military. Reforming these institutions, the object of many recommendations, would go far towards building a culture of human rights and strengthening the rule of law. It goes without saying that truth commissions themselves cannot reform institutions or effect policy changes; nor do they have the power to bring perpetrators to trial. As Hayner notes "[a commission] must depend on the political will and interest of the government for its recommendations to be given force."[49]

Transitional justice is not mainstreamed
While the use of truth-telling exercises continues to expand to new areas around the world—the first truth commissions in both the United States and Middle East were established within six months of each other in 2004—the mainstreaming of scholarship has not kept apace. Almost all literature on transitional justice has been published in English or Spanish. Governments and human rights NGOs in the French- and Arabic-speaking worlds thus have little access to information about other cases. Bickford notes that the term "transitional justice" and the meanings behind it do not translate well into other languages.[50] Freeman argues that the field is overwhelmingly Anglocentric, both in its writings and in its experts.[51] If transitional justice is to become increasingly globalized, money and expertise is needed to translate reports, academic writings, and other documents, so that the lessons learned in one area of the world can be applied elsewhere.

Conclusion

In the past few decades a paradigmatic model of truth telling has emerged, one that is so taken for granted that it is difficult to imagine a scenario in which a country that has recently undergone a transition from dictatorship to democracy or from governance through repression to a human rights—respecting rule of law does not create some mechanism—or, increasingly, mechanisms-for uncovering the facts about past violations. Disclosure of "the Truth" as a constitutive element of a just and lasting peace has simply become standard operating procedure. Much is known about what works and what does not work in terms of truth telling and peacebuilding; yet much also remains unknown. Countries attempting to apply one or more transitional justice mechanisms often face a serious challenge: just when the need or demand for justice is at its highest, the ability to deliver it may be at its lowest, often due to a combination of low political will and a lack of capacity to deliver.[52]

And yet, victims and survivors of former rights-abusing regimes have shown that they will not be thwarted in their quest for justice, accountability, and recognition. A key group among these victims and survivors—as well as among the perpetrators—is youth. It is to youth, then, than the next chapter turns. In general, there is every reason to believe that the transitional justice project will be around for a long time to come and will continue to evolve as new experiments—driven by ever-changing contexts of violence—become incorporated into standard practices.

CHAPTER 4

Caught between Child Rights and Security: Youth and Postwar Reconstruction

For the most part, the gap between child victims and power structures is terra incognita, occupied by neither child rights activists nor security analysts. What then, will ensure the political rights of young people and the protection of their political space against incursion? [1]

Introduction

Forty-six percent of the world's population is under age twenty-four. In the last decade, there has been an increase in absolute numbers of young people, even though as a proportion of global population, the numbers of youth have declined in every region except Africa. Concentrated in the developing world, and particularly in Africa and in Asia, youth in many countries constitute the majority of their populations. Some country-specific numbers further illustrate this point. According to United Nations research,[2] the percentage of the population aged under twenty-four in Iraq is 60 percent.[3] In Afghanistan and the Occupied Palestinian Territories, 65 percent are under twenty-four.[4] Similar percentages are found in countries across Africa. In Côte d'Ivoire, for example, 64 percent of the population is aged under twenty-four.[5] In Sierra Leone, 60 percent are in this age-group.[6] In South Africa, the number is 50 percent under twenty-four.[7] Sizeable minorities of youth are the picture in Northern Ireland, Sri Lanka, and Israel, where 30–40 percent are under twenty-four.[8] Yet, even where youth are the majorities in their societies, they often perceive themselves as "outcast minorities."[9] In fact, they are more likely than their elders to lack access to resources and essential services and to be excluded from social and political processes and institutions.

Large numbers of youth, while seemingly correlated with sociopolitical violence in a number of studies (see "youth bulge" theories discussed below), do
not in themselves explain or predict armed conflict. A fluid and interactive
combination of grievances, coercion, need, opportunity, subjective interpretations, and narratives drive the involvement of youth in the cycle of contemporary wars. To understand the full range of pressures that influence and mitigate
youth involvement in armed conflict, it is necessary to use a number of different disciplinary lenses, bridging child rights advocacy and security analysis, to
explore the diverse environments in which youth live and their everyday experiences and ideas. The contributors to the RIREC volume *Troublemakers or
Peacemakers?*[10] show that youth, whether majorities or minorities in their populations, participate in armed conflict because of economic, social, and political
exclusion, threats to identity, layers of trauma, and direct and indirect experience of a variety of forms of violence and displacement. Youth are as often the
victims as they are the perpetrators of violence in ongoing wars and after conflict. A further frequently ignored facet of the relationship of youth to war is
that, everywhere there is armed conflict, young people participate in mitigating
its effects through grassroots community building, organized peace work, and
more hidden daily interactions with peers and families and within other networks.[11] A key lesson learned is that postwar peacebuilding efforts will need to
appreciate and address this complexity and that every context is different. With
this basic foundation, the purpose of this chapter is to present some general
findings about youth issues, roles, and needs in postwar situations.

In postwar periods, traditional structures and/or key institutions—education, health, or recreation, for example—that might protect young people, mitigate youth violence, and productively channel youth energies, are often
nonexistent or fragile. Where children and youth have experienced the power
of carrying arms, political promises in recruitment, and positive self-concepts
and identity in armed conflict, the transition to "peace" is very difficult and
intergenerational conflict is likely in postwar phases. Even if youth have been
actively involved in political activism and political violence before a settlement
they now become marginal, as political power flows to adult leadership, elders,
or external international power elites. But parental, elder, and external authority may be disputed. Often, youth grievances from before the war can be linked
to repressive or unfair systems of local governance and resource distribution
which remain unchanged postwar or, in some cases, are actively reproduced
through donor aid efforts.[12] Likewise, re-opening schools, while essential, may
not address the needs of older youth, and teachers may be distrusted[13] and/or
they may be distrustful of their students. The questions, criticisms, and creativity of youth are often not rewarded or fostered in these contexts.[14] Conflicts
emerge when adults try to curb both youth violence and peace activism.[15]

Moreover, various forms of state-sponsored and factional violence continue
to target youth, both directly and indirectly, and gangs and community defense

organizations and militias develop with marginal youth at their centers. War-related trauma is widespread and the practical difficulties of economic survival compound it, creating new grievances. New conflicts threaten from outside, as regional wars and rumors of war persist. Many of the same problems experienced during and before war remain, yet they take on a new meaning. In a muddled zone of new hope and old grievances, a peace process, transition, or reconstruction period is a powerful symbol as well as a lived experience. Such a period raises expectations. As both symbol and experience, it shape attitudes and values; young people's interpretations of its relative costs and benefits form an important test of its legitimacy and sustainability. Over time, more and more people may move into the spoiler camps. Cycles of violence are related to the vulnerability and marginality of youth as well as their roles as social connectors and ideological reproducers, who create and shape social meaning. But, equally important, these social networks of youth offer existing and potential peace roles. Youth have a multidimensional impact in postwar situations. They also have multidimensional needs which argue for holistic interventions-particularly economic, psychosocial, educational, and political inclusion-that utilize the knowledge of youth and cede some significant political power to them.

Youth Roles in War and Peace: Frameworks and Approaches

The term "youth" can encompass a lot in terms of age and experience. Moreover, in post-conflict situations, the characteristics of the conflict and conflict resolution landscape are so interwoven that to analyze and prescribe for sustainable peace it is helpful to draw on the insights offered by a number of different, though overlapping, literatures. The first section of this chapter, although not an exhaustive review, discusses some of the main concerns, findings, and trends within the rights-based children-in-armed-conflict literature, the psychological-impact-of-war literature, and the security, development, and education literatures. It argues that in considering youth strategies in post-conflict situations, it is important to integrate what is already known about children, youth, war, and peace into a hybrid framework for analysis and policy implementation. Though acknowledging that a hybrid peacebuilding approach may in fact be more useful for analysis than for policy, the chapter offers concrete recommendations in specific areas and applies them to an existing tool for organizing reconstruction methods on the ground.

Children in armed conflict

There is a large literature on child soldiers and children in armed conflict[16] that has investigated how and why child soldiers are recruited to armed groups, the demobilization and rehabilitation challenges and programmatic efforts, and the effects of war-related displacement on children. This literature also, more generally, identifies human rights abuses and prescribes for the safety, health, and development rights and needs of all war-affected children.[17] Scholars have shown that as well as being a large percentage of the casualties of war, children and youth have a variety of other roles as active combatants—both forced and voluntary—spies, weapons couriers, mine-clearers, cooks, and forced "wives." As this literature has evolved, the special situation of adolescents, girls, disabled children, AIDS orphans in war zones, and children born of wartime rape have emerged as important areas for further research and programmatic response.[18] A significant number of country-specific studies written by psychologists and anthropologists[19] have given depth to the breadth of United Nations and NGO studies and advocacy reports, and together this literature has had two important impacts. First, it has made child fighters around the world visible, highlighted multiple violations of their rights and welfare, and placed them on the global humanitarian agenda. Second, although the overall picture is one in which children are exploited by the architects of war, this literature also has profoundly challenged the notion that children and youth are victims or perpetrators of violence only. Dispelling monolithic images of child soldiers and young refugees, these authors provide many examples of the resilience of youth in war zones and the morally complex choices they make and roles they play.

Most recently, the literature has emphasized the complex interplay of factors and critical choice points that bring children into combat[20] and the multidimensional unfolding of the experience of war and related displacement in the lives of children and adolescents, including how war experience can stimulate creativity, community building, and the development of multiple competencies and caretaking roles.[21] However, although the UN does have a youth program oriented towards fifteen- to twenty-four-year-olds, the vast literature on child soldiers and children in armed conflict takes the under-eighteen age-group as its focus point for the most part. This has had the effect of raising awareness about children in war but has left study of youth primarily to security analysts (as will be discussed below). A second problem is one of policy rather than the literature. Practical implementation of effective measures to prevent and/or punish child soldiering have been lacking to date.[22] In July 2005, the UN Security Council unanimously passed Resolution 1612 describing a "lack of overall progress on the ground" in eradicating the use of child soldiers and announcing "an era of application."[23] The resolution established the UN's first comprehensive monitoring and reporting program. But enforcing compliance of laws prohibiting child soldiering will require further action by the Security Council in response to reports generated by this mechanism.

Psychological impact of war on children

The children-in-armed-conflict literature, which emphasizes legal and psychosocial issues, builds on an older body of work dating from the Second World War on the psychological effects of conflict on children.[24] This literature investigates the long-term impact of wartime trauma on children, their coping mechanisms, their political socialization, and how children and young people conceptualize war and peace.[25] It shows that children are alert to their political surroundings from a very early age with perceptions of "the other" developing from around age three.[26] Early trauma manifests itself in a variety of negative ways but children are also resilient, especially if parental or other support systems are available. Children's experience of conflict is complex, and not always as negative as adults perceive.[27] These psychological studies also contribute important understandings of the long-term, trans-generational sharing of trauma and attitudes that contribute to cycles of violence. But while most of these studies take cautious views and are often reluctant to prescribe policy, overall they are hopeful about the ability of children to survive wartime trauma and become productive citizens postwar.[28]

Security studies
In security studies, there are two converging trends. The first security-based approach focuses on the relationship between "youth bulges" and the likelihood of civil war. These studies suggest that countries with 40 percent or more of a population aged between fifteen and twenty-nine are demographic time bombs, with a 2.5 times higher risk of civil war than other countries.[29] The second trend, since 2001, has been related to the "war on terror," which has prompted U.S. military strategists to more specifically strategize for child soldiers[30] and to examine the impact that child soldiering has on how wars are fought and how long they last.[31] The convergence of these approaches is well illustrated in the following:

> From continent to continent and across race and religion, the "demographic" of insurgency, ethnic conflict, terrorism, and state-sponsored violence holds constant. The vast majority of recruits are young men, most of them out of school and out of work. It is a formula that hardly varies, whether in the scattered hideouts of Al Qaeda, on the backstreets of Baghdad or Port-au-Prince, or in the rugged mountains of Macedonia, Chechnya, Afghanistan, or eastern Colombia. . . . In these regions, where average family size tends to be large, boys grow up in youth-packed neighborhoods where parental authority in the home can take a back seat to the power of adolescent males on the streets.[32]

Critics of the security approach note a tendency towards monolithic views of male youth as threats, a deterministic view that where there are young males (especially in cities in the developing world) there *will* be violence.[33] Moreover, a number of scholars take issue with the assumption of youth bulge analysts that urbanization, gender, and population pressure are more important in predicting violence than how resources are distributed and the impact of foreign aid.[34] Policy recommendations in security studies favor economic investment and family planning or population control. U.S. military strategists have emphasized the special preparation and post-combat counseling that U.S. forces need

before and after facing child soldiers, the public relations implications of this
kind of combat, the importance of using U.S. forces to protect child-soldier
demobilization centers, and the need for further development and deployment
of nonlethal weapons in fighting wars against child soldiers.[35] Points of tension
exist with other approaches in that the securitization of youth (and children)
suggests an increasing emphasis on them as threats or risks rather than as victims or active agents for peace. Others express concern that the war on terror
tends to draw funding away from places of extreme need, such as West Africa,
and from holistic approaches to child and youth needs.[36]

Development
The development literature overlaps with the security literature, the education
literature (below), and the children-in-armed-conflict literature. The greed or
grievance debate[37] intersects with the youth bulge findings; these analysts share
a focus on issues of economic investment in youth, economic incentives to pull
youth away from armed conflict, strategies for youth employment, HIV/AIDS,
and concern about demographic explosions in developing countries. However,
where children and youth are concerned, the development literature emphasizes a broader set of concerns ranging from early childhood health and nutri-
tion, lifelong education, youth substance abuse, and child labor, as well as youth
and violence.[38] Moreover, the development approach especially emphasizes
youth participation and intergenerational relations. And as the former president
of the World Bank, James Wolfensohn, states, the World Bank applies the same
"capacity-building" approach to post-conflict peacebuilding as to development
in non-conflict contexts.[39] A key element of that approach is the notion of
youth "empowerment," where youth are viewed "as a human asset, a medium-
long term investment for creating thriving societies, and a base for social capital development."[40] There is a vast literature critiquing and evaluating both the
ethics and the practice of development aid in conflict zones,[41] which will not
be reviewed here. Suffice to say that economic and social development are
essential elements of post-conflict peacebuilding and are fraught with dilemmas
and difficulties, some of which will be discussed later in this chapter.

Education in conflict zones
The conflict and peace education literatures explore the relationship between
violent conflict and education access, education systems, and curriculum.[42] This
literature also analyzes and prescribes roles for education in promoting social
cohesion and peace. It has contributed important understandings about how
education can create social division and how "inequities and inadequacies within the education system can push young people towards conflict."[43] While education is vital for the economic development of stable societies, education
systems also can reproduce inequality, militarism, and constructions of "the
other" that create conflict.[44] However, education also has a vital role in foster-

ing peace. Margaret Sinclair summarizes the importance of education in emergencies (crisis and post-crisis):

- education can help meet the psychosocial needs of crisis-affected populations
- education provides a channel for conveying survival messages and developing skills for conflict resolution and peacebuilding
- education is needed to prepare for reconstruction, and social and economic development
- education can provide protection from harm
- education is a human right, promoting personal development and preparedness for responsible citizenship.[45]

This literature highlights the need for ensuring access to education (recognizing the special barriers against girls, disabled children, and other minority children getting to school), for good coordination and planning, and for using a long time frame. It also emphasizes the development of specific skills and values as peace productive. The UNESCO "Learning to Live Together" initiative expresses this agenda and is focused on "the development of understanding, consideration, and respect for others, their beliefs, values and cultures . . . to provide the basis for the avoidance of conflicts or their nonviolent resolution and for ongoing peaceful coexistence."[46] Emphasis is placed on integrated life-skills programs that teach skills such as handling emotions, empathetic listening and other communication skills, mediation, critical thinking, problem solving, relationship building, and, most recently, community service projects.[47] Moreover, it is recognized that beyond reopening schools in post-conflict situations, it is necessary to pay attention to what is being taught and how. Teacher training, pedagogy, and textbooks are coming under increasing scrutiny as components of a pro-peace or pro-violence education. There appears to be a trend towards emphasizing civic or citizenship education as opposed to human rights or peace education, as the latter can be perceived to serve some conflict groups more than others or to be part of a "pacification" project. From the conflict education literature and practice also comes an emphasis on fostering youth as change agents for peace through informal peer education, networking, participation at all levels of society, and training in information technology, project management, and conflict negotiation and resolution.[48] Education in nontraditional settings as well as in schools is being seen as essential for reaching wider spheres of youth. Some also see a key role for education in fostering critical evaluation of the past as a step that will lead to wider societal healing and reconciliation.[49] As Jeffrey Helsing has noted, an important peacebuilding opportunity exists in integrating lessons from official truth and reconciliation processes into school history courses and in the teaching of history in general.[50]

Post-conflict situations and youth
The literature on post-conflict reconstruction and peacebuilding focused specifically on youth (as opposed to education) is still not extensive. It consists of a small number of broad-ranging academic studies, some country-specific studies, and NGO, UN, and government aid-agency reports.[51] Scholars lag behind aid agencies and international organizations in only beginning to address such questions as: What role do/should children and youth have in peace negotiations/processes, or in the implementation of peace accords? How do children and youth impact the sustainability of peace?[52] There is scant interdisciplinary research or even synthesis of relevant research concentrated on youth as actors in post-conflict situations. Neither has there been a focus on youth in the conflict prevention literature. One problem posed by Angela McIntrye (and quoted at the beginning of this chapter) is that youth—perhaps, especially, older adolescents and those older than eighteen—fall into a contested area between child rights activists and security analysts. Briefly, in the children-in-armed-conflict approach, the child is first a person to be protected and then assured a broad range of nonnegotiable rights. In the security approach, a youth is a threat to be fought, contained, or bought off with economic incentives. The focus of each approach—rights or security—shapes who is viewed and how. A fuller picture of youth in war and postwar requires the development lens, which adds an emphasis on youth empowerment through participation and attention to whole life cycles; the lens of psychological impact, which identifies trauma and subjective meaning as central to the reproduction of cycles of violence; and the education lens, which shows the importance of educational structures, practice, and ethos in shaping the practical opportunities and long-term values of youth. So, the challenge in post-conflict contexts seems to be to further combine and integrate these analytical lenses and to build on what is already known about children and youth and about good practice.

In this regard, the value of a hybrid peacebuilding framework lies in its transdisciplinary aspirations and its focus on post-conflict reconstruction as a process involving mitigation and containment of violence, addressing root causes of violence, and transforming conflict relationships.[53] McEvoy-Levy et al. considered youth within such a hybrid peacebuilding framework in *Troublemakers or Peacemakers?*[54] From a variety of disciplinary perspectives, the contributors to the volume analyzed the roles of youth in post-accord environments in overlapping categories of victims/perpetrators, violence production/peace production, and conflict reproduction/conflict transformation. Hence, it was possible to see the problem of youth along a conflict trajectory in four interrelated ways:

1. Originating in the roles and experience of youth prewar and during war as victims, perpetrators, and displaced people;
2. Evolving into the roles and experience of youth transitioning from war. These roles include membership in criminal gangs, militias, and parapo-

litical militant organizations or as recreational or accidental spoilers whose alienation and apathy has impact on the legitimacy and sustainability of peace;

3. Involving as well the roles and experience of youth in nonviolent politics, peace organizing, and other post-militant activism, including organic community building and ideological reproduction and/or transformation; and

4. Including the roles, experiences, and aspirations of youth involved in methods for dealing with the past and transitional justice.

This approach showed the multidimensional force and impact of youth on the problem of postwar peacebuilding, specifically on violence prevention, on the legitimacy of any negotiated settlement, and on the sustainability of peace. The volume's authors also identified youth's multidimensional needs that argue for complex holistic interventions.[55]

The next section outlines the dilemmas and lessons learned from this study, and from other recent studies focused on issues of youth in post-conflict situations. Then it applies these insights to an existing implementation tool, a "Reconstruction Matrix," to examine what hybrid peacebuilding analysis has to offer on the ground in complex conflicts.

Youth and Postwar Peacebuilding: Dilemmas and Lessons Learned
A hybrid peacebuilding approach, described above, is the framework for the eight themes explored below, each of which relate to the dilemmas and policy implications of youth in post-conflict situations.

Who are youth?
In analyzing the roles and needs of youth in postwar situations, the first issue to address is who are youth in a given context? The answers to this question obviously vary across cases. For example, in one context people equate youth with adolescents. In other contexts, such as in many African countries, youth are aged twelve to thirty-five or even forty. The United Nations definition is fifteen to twenty-four, which overlaps with the international legal category of the child, which is anyone under eighteen.[56] Youth bulge theorists and security analysts focus on fifteen- to twenty-nine-year-olds. In *Troublemakers or Peacemakers?*, the framework used was ages twelve to thirty, in order to apply the widest analytical lens for understanding the social, political, economic, and military agency of youth. It would seem most appropriate and effective to follow local cultures in each individual case, but adding to the complexity of the problem, there are cases where local people may decide on a definition that does not have a basis in culture but instead suits a political moment. For example, Andrew Mawson describes how some Acholi combatants in Uganda were rehabilitated through the perpetuation of the "collective fiction" that *all* combatants were "children" and hence lacked moral responsibility for their actions. In this case, reconceptu-

alizations of childhood were utilized to absolve older youth and adults and thus advance reconstruction and reconciliation efforts, though the long-term outcomes of this strategy remain uncertain.[57]

Policy makers and aid providers face decisions about whether to follow an international or local definition and/or whether to prioritize a particular cohort, such as adolescents, or those identified as particularly "at risk," such as ex-combatants. There are multiple difficulties in how youth are defined, and some opportunities, too. Too-flexible definitions of youth (going up to age thirty, for example) may make programming difficult. At the same time, interventions that serve too-tight definitions may also prove ineffective or create conflict. For example, Liza Sekaggya states that some girl soldiers in Uganda were not admitted to NGO rehabilitation centers because they were nineteen, just past the cut-off age of eighteen. Where an ex-combatant is also caring for her children, as was the case in Sekaggya's report, the strict criterion influenced by international law may negatively impact two generations.[58] As well, the very mechanisms that seek to rehabilitate ex-combatants—such as demobilization, disarmament, and reintegration (DDR) programs—can have the effect of alienating other youth who don't qualify.[59] This may reinforce notions that violence pays. Since notions of "youth" are not static in any context, it may make sense for scholars and practitioners to think critically and flexibly about how youth are defined, although this is not without its difficulties for policy. Some organizations, for example, have expressed concern about moving beyond a specific program such as DDR to include other youth, because it would expand a commitment and make exit difficult.[60]

Yet, on the opportunities side, attention to the different categories (and definitions) of youth in any conflict situation provides a more complete picture of their different needs—without which youth programs and strategies can be less effective and even do harm. For example, even the category "ex-combatant" has a number of sublevels: male and female ex-combatants, ex-combatants with children (child mothers), abducted versus voluntary recruits, ideologically versus economically motivated recruits. And these ex-combatants can be distinguished from noncombatant youth who are also without education or job skills and may have been displaced. The length of time a young person spends in displacement or as a recruit is also a significant factor in rehabilitation. Special needs groups such as youth with HIV/AIDS, children born into armed groups, children and youth with disabilities, and survivors of sexual violence form additional subcategories. At the same time, as will be argued further below, there is often not a stark division between combatants and ex-combatants.

The problem of youth violence after war is layered and complex.
Youth violence after war is not easily categorized or tackled as it is motivated by a combination of factors: being a victim of violence (of different kinds); lack of access to education, land, or employment; trauma; subjective meanings; pow-

erful images and narratives; and political exclusion. Clearly, which factors combine, and how, is different in each case of conflict, and even for each individual involved. How, then, can effective violence prevention policy be implemented? Where does youth violence fit into spoiler practice? Is it intentional spoiling behavior or recreational spoiling—where intentionality is unclear but the outcome destabilizing? How does one categorize demobilized children and youth who are reabducted into armed groups when peace agreements collapse—hostage spoilers? Are there special issues related to DDR and youth?

DDR is priority one in peace accord implementation. In the long term, DDR is conceived of as a mechanism for social transformation. In the short term, it is often a political tool to lubricate a peace negotiation. These can be contradictory, or at least competing, aims, especially as applied to youth. At the early stages of a peace process, demobilizing young soldiers can be both a political embarrassment—for both the exploiters of child soldiers and those who fight against them—and, perhaps, evidence for war crimes prosecutions. In Mozambique in 1999, the conflict parties tacitly agreed to deny the existence of child soldiers. When this happens, young combatants are effectively re-marginalized in ceasefire and early settlement negotiations. Practically, they are left out of the DDR process; ironically, their political importance is the reason for the attempt to render them politically meaningless—invisible in terms of a peace settlement.

Even where child soldiers are demobilized early, peace process politics can negatively shape their treatment, as reported by the UN about Burundi: ". . . many children formerly associated with armed groups were cantoned in assembly areas where they waited for over eight months to return to their families; this delay was due to the lack of commitment of some leaders, lengthy negotiations over global demobilization and inadequate disarmament, demobilization and reintegration resources." [61]

Moreover, youth who have previously been soldiers are trained assets and therefore attractive to armed groups when peace accords fail, as in Sierra Leone in 1999. The availability of these children was ensured by their vulnerable status as ex-combatants, many of them internally displaced and without protection, and underlines the importance of swift and effective (re)integration in breaking cycles of violence. In cases like these, the spoilers are not the child or youth foot soldiers themselves, but rebel commanders. Yet political necessity or expedience brings these same leaders into peace talks, often offering immunity from prosecution, and therefore no disincentive to capture children again if a further round of hostilities takes place. The 2005 indictment of Lord's Resistance Army (LRA) commander Joseph Kony by the International Criminal Court, despite concerns about its impact on the negotiations between the LRA and the Ugandan government, is an interesting departure. But, noting the dilemmas involved, the head of the Ugandan Amnesty Commission said it would make it harder for other rebel fighters to come into a peace process.[62]

The challenge facing the United Nations DDR program and UNICEF in Afghanistan is also instructive. An estimated 100,000 ex-combatants will need to be reintegrated by the UN's Afghanistan New Beginnings Program. Eight thousand children in armed groups are being addressed by a separate UNICEF child soldier demobilization and reintegration program. Over 3,820 of these children had been demobilized in late 2004, and the reintegration portion of the program began in October 2005.[63] In the postwar period in Afghanistan, law and order is being enforced by ex-combatants from the Northern Alliance, and these include children. One thirteen-year-old with a Kalashnikov rifle found directing traffic at a Kabul intersection stated: "I came to Kabul when my brothers [in the Northern Alliance] removed the Taliban. Before I was in a camp, but now I'm a policeman and proud."[64] The transitioning of youth from war fighting to postwar security roles creates another policy dilemma. Following international law, the Afghan government has banned the use of child soldiers in the new Afghan National Army and is reported to be removing under-seventeens from the force. However, this will certainly rankle with adolescents who fought in the war against the Taliban, but are now excluded from new security institutions, making very good integration imperative.

A former youth combatant in the Democratic Republic of Congo (DRC), who gave his gun to the UN and was paid $50, puts the problem this way: "We are disappointed, because when we disarmed, they promised to help us with projects and finding some work. But up until now, we haven't been helped. And this is risky because we have friends who are still in the bush. They are watching what happens to us. They are waiting to see if we are helped before they decide whether to disarm or not."[65] In DRC in 2005, elections were held up because while 15,000 combatants had been demobilized by the UN, 1,200 militia members in the northeast refused to disarm, showing how small numbers have quite large consequences.

Even if original hostilities do not resume, ex-combatants are more vulnerable to recruitment into other forms of armed groups, such as criminal gangs. Youth in postwar situations have the opportunity to earn substantial sums of money through crime and vigilantism, and given the economic instability and hardships of a postwar period, this is a tempting career path. But, as Wessells and Jonah discovered, some would choose much smaller incomes, "respect" in their communities, and "positive social roles" if presented with those opportunities. "The stipends really helped," noted one ex-combatant youth who was a participant in an NGO rehabilitation program in Sierra Leone. Another stated, "After the ceasefire, I had no gun and got no package [that is, did not qualify for the government benefits for former soldiers]. Now we are presentable and can survive . . . Before we had only cassava but now we have rice—this makes us believe in peace."[66] As the case of the Afghan child "proud" to be directing traffic also showed, youth will seek out positive social roles and respect in their communities.

In ethnic and national liberation conflicts, local communities sustain and politicize youth during conflict, and often protect them in militarized enclaves. But, after accords, these same communities restrict or attempt to restrict young peoples' violence and often their political and peace agency also. At the same time, the protective enclave is worn away. An experience of being defenseless and powerless seems to ensue for some. In Northern Ireland, youth involvement in recreational rioting causes paramilitary actors to walk a fine line between controlling the escalation of violence and, at the same time, maintaining enough respect in their communities to later "turn on" community violence if political-ly necessary. And youth express confusion about the roles they should play in conflict politics.[67]

A key post-conflict challenge is to provide opportunities for youth to tran-sition into nonmilitary roles (as well as military roles, such as integration into a new police force) that involve community service. Integrating under-eighteens into new security institutions is undesirable on a number of levels. But a peace and reconstruction corps of some kind to provide youth with livelihood skills training as well as a means to serve community needs may be desirable in some contexts. Such institutions would allow youth to positively express the strong "ethic of community loyalty"[68] that is often developed in armed conflict.

There are further layers to the problem of youth violence. Domestic and gender-based violence pose a particularly tough problem because they are usu-ally considered private rather than public concerns, and can remain hidden in conflict analyses. Yet, in many recruitment stories, domestic and sexual violence before and after recruitment are prominent. For example: "People say that we're a problem, but they don't know our problems. My uncle raped me when I was 12 and I joined the rebels because I thought it would be better having sex with strangers instead of people in my family. Now the war is over, we have put down our guns, and I am working as a prostitute because I can't get another job. No one really cares about us."[69]

Certainly, much more official emphasis in peace processes can be placed on preventing domestic and sexual violence, through implementing grassroots edu-cation efforts and gender-sensitive human rights training for the police and mil-itary. The recruitment stories in Boxes 4.1 and 4.2 suggest the importance of childhood domestic violence along with poverty, displacement, and lack of access to education. These factors make youth vulnerable to powerful forces organizing for war and underline how a policy implementing children's human rights should have a central place in postwar reconstruction efforts designed to break cycles of violence.

Box 4.1: Chronological Dimensions of a Recruitment Narrative
Javad, Afghan militant, age 15
- Disrupted family life—loss of father
- Intrusion of war
- Lack of access to education
- Family displacement
- Poverty
- Domestic violence
- Religious education
- Displacement again—due to inability to pay for religious education
- Lack of income
- Critical choice point when the absence of alternatives leads to joining a nonviolent political organization
- Later joins armed group related to that organization.

Source: Summarized from Brett and Sprecht, *Young Soldiers*, 78–79.

Box 4.2: Chronological Dimensions of a Recruitment Narrative
Gaspar, Guatemalan Army Recruit, age 16
- Given away by his mother at age six (for economic reasons) to owner of a coffee farm
- Beaten by farm owner
- Returns home to domestic violence—beaten by stepfather
- Prejudice because "we were Indians"
- Suicide attempt
- Domestic violence again
- Second suicide attempt
- Displacement—lives on streets
- Survives by digging through garbage, begging, and stealing
- Drug use
- Third suicide attempt
- Further experience of prejudice—feels "humiliation"
- Avoids army recruiters
- Finally "allows" army to catch him so he can "learn to read and write" and "for shoes."

Source: Summarized from Sanford, "Moral Imagination of Survival," 57–59.

Postwar peacebuilding initiatives need to accommodate the fact that the reasons youth became involved in armed conflict in the first place differ substantially "according to the situation, gender, the armed group one is with, one's mode of entry, and individual skills and competencies in negotiating one's role within the situation and group."[70] An important lesson learned is the need to identify as many of these complexities as possible. Governments and organizations developing programs and policies for youth in post-conflict situations should use local expertise to do a complete analysis of the impact of the conflict on youth and of the impact youth have had on the conflict.

Tangible gains for youth are a litmus test for a sustainable peace process.
Displacement, physical insecurity, and restricted access to education, employment, land, and capital make it difficult to move beyond the past. Tangible gains for youth in these areas are a litmus test for the legitimacy and sustainability of a peace or transition process. At noted above, displacement is often one of the first events from which participation in armed conflicts unfolds.[71] A key task is to avoid new cycles of displacement and to promote reintegration: returning youth to their homes or communities—if possible and desired by youth—or integrating them into new communities. Because the notion of reintegration may be flawed, consultation with youth is vital. As Marc Sommers points out: "The backward glance inferred by reintegration may be precisely what many people, youth in particular, do not want."[72]

The prevention of violence against youth by the state, external actors, internal organized armed groups, community militias, street gangs, or random sectarianism is another priority because attacks on youth can stimulate re-recruitment or transitioning to gangs for protection. Physical insecurity also works against acceptance of a settlement which, to be sustainable, has to be perceived to have provided a better life. So, a particularly vigorous approach to protecting the physical safety and human rights of youth in demobilization centers, refugee camps, on the street, and in detention is warranted. In most postwar contexts, a children's and young people's rights approach would demonstrate a clear break from the past, provide a pro-peace, pro-human rights education for the next generation, and work against cycles of redemptive violence.

Likewise, access to education, skills training, employment, and options for positive roles in community life are the other most urgent needs of youth moving out of war. Lessons from the field point to early planning to insure that ex-combatant skills-training matches the labor market and that DDR programs include start-up funds or other means of effective transition into sustainable employment. Michael Wessells and Davidson Jonah, Sommers, Jaco Cilliers, and others suggest that the kind of youth strategies necessary to build sustainable peace entail close local consultation, careful planning, a broad scope, and a long-term commitment. As one young Bosnian states: "In addition to an improved economy and education system, peace building needs to be sustained and rewarded. If lives do not improve, there will be little faith in peace. . . . young people question whether the international community has the power or desire to bring about positive changes. Too often, it seems, the rhetoric and the monetary pledges do not make a difference on the ground."[73]

When peace or transition processes become protracted and implementation of agreements contentious, a new generation of youth that has not experienced war may come to disrespect local leaders or international peace brokers, and become impatient with their politics. Youth apathy and/or increasing extremism impacts electoral results and stability on the ground, as has been noted recently in Northern Ireland, Bosnia, and Kosovo.

Moreover, it is also clear that even youth who did not participate in armed struggle can still develop militarized identities, aversions to democratic dialogue, hard-line political attitudes, and support for authoritarian solutions.[74] And war weariness might not apply to these young people. In the medium to long term, the fact that some youth have not experienced actual combat but have grown up in a divided, politically violent, sectarian, or repressive society may make them more likely than others to acquiesce to political or military forces that seek to reignite violence, especially if they perceive few tangible gains from peace.

Traumatic memory, subjective meaning, and symbolism must be addressed.
In post-conflict situations, two of the fundamental barriers to moving beyond the past are the trauma of individuals involved in or impacted by violence and also the collective trauma of the society within which there is a widespread sense of powerlessness, hopelessness, and distrust, and a lack of confidence in a settlement's endurance or its ability to effect real transformation. These findings suggest that traumatic memory, subjective meaning, and conflict symbolism should be addressed in ways that actively involve youth in narrative building and meaning making.

Traumatic memories interact with subjective interpretations of threat and history, deeply held beliefs, and evocative symbols that youth both receive as an inheritance and create themselves.[75] As shown in Box 4.3, young women in Northern Ireland justified their involvement in sectarian street fighting and riots after the Good Friday Agreement with a number of different subjective interpretations of threats to physical person, territory, and both personal and collective identities.

Box 4.3: Different Explanations of Involvement In Riots Young Women in Northern Ireland, ages 12–18.
- Territorial threat of the ethnic other
- Recreation—*I love riotin.' It's fun.* *
- Youth vanguard—leading part of community effort
- *Peaceful protest*
- Self-defense against police
- Economic inequalities/exclusion
- Vulnerability of children in general
- Personal vulnerability
- Religious identity—*Why do they believe in Holy Mary? [Because] they never grew up.*
- Religious/apocalyptic—*I can see the world coming to war.*
- Inevitability of cycles of violence
- Political exclusion—*No one listens to us.*

* *Italics* signify direct quotes.

Source: Summarized from McEvoy-Levy, "Politics, Protest and Local 'Power-Sharing,'" 139–71.

Addressing practical things such as violence, education, and unemployment in ways that do not account for the specific meanings—both personal and collective—that youth attach to the experience of violence or a peace process may be less effective, and perhaps even counterproductive. It is important to understand how, from their own authentic experiences, young people conceptualize the problems that confront them.[76] Narrative construction is organic to the everyday activities and interactions of youth and part of a process of peer education. The stories youth tell in school, street, gang, refugee camp, or other organization shape and are shaped by more organized narratives such murals and graffiti, Internet sites, blogs, songs, poems, and political pamphlets, which young people also participate in creating. In these ways youth can have a central role in the reproduction of conflicts. Through the narratives that they create and share with each other they may reproduce (or help perpetuate) the larger conflict by passing on old reasons for war or by creating new explanations for why it is necessary to fight.

Yet, youth also create narratives in these formats that are supportive of peace. How is it possible to utilize youth's knowledge as well as norm-building and peer-education roles to address trauma and subjective meaning—and, more generally, as peacebuilding tools? Among the lessons learned are that, in some contexts, indigenous, local healing and reconciliation methods that involve public ritual[77] are preferable to individualized talk-therapy models. Another important psychological finding is that political leadership and a sense of political purpose may inoculate young people against trauma.[78] Storytelling—which may be oral, text-based, art- or theatre-based, personal, local, or national-has broad basis in world cultures and appeal as means for equalizing and even reconciling conflicting views of the past, and for healing dialogue.[79]

The research suggests that whatever transitional justice model is chosen (and, as the previous chapter in this volume shows, a number of options exist), youth should be closely and publicly engaged in it. Truth commissions, for example, should involve youth, not only in providing testimonies, but also in the day-to-day organization of submissions and in writing final reports. Likewise, other mechanisms for dealing with the past, such as media retrospectives, museums, and memorials, should involve youth in collecting and compiling stories and designing installations. Allowing youth to achieve political authority through providing them with authorial roles is a way to address apathy and disillusionment, and a form of active youth political participation that is usually lacking in postwar contexts.

Postwar political marginalization of youth undermines peace.
For a variety of reasons-principled, pragmatic, and ideological-youth are politically marginalized in post-conflict situations; that is, as an age-group they are marginalized more than others of their faction or ethnic, racial, religious, or national group. The international community has yet to seriously implement policies for youth political participation.

This political exclusion reverberates particularly negatively where young people have had active roles in combat before a ceasefire.[80] Like experience of post-conflict violence, political exclusion impacts young people's attitudes towards a peace agreement or transition process. Common among youth are perceptions of their irrelevance to how political processes unfold:

> People don't listen to us . . . Our opinion? The government would rip that up and throw it in the bin. THEY don't care. . . . People don't believe in what young people have to say. (Northern Ireland)

> Decisions are made for us by people who do not have an idea of what we are faced with on a daily basis. (Bosnia)

> When one is displaced, one loses the feeling of being . . . a citizen with rights and responsibilities. (Guatemala)[81]

Child rights activists, although often committed to furthering participation rights, prioritize a "return to childhood." Security analysts, remarkably, although focused on much older population, usually fifteen- to twenty-nine-year-olds, usually do not recommend youth political participation as a useful policy, even though some recommend encouraging women's participation.

The United Nations World Youth Report and Security Council Resolution 1379 both note the desirability of the participation of children and youth in certain circumstances in relation to post-conflict reintegration (emphasis in the original): **"The issues pertinent to the situation of youth and former child soldiers should be incorporated into peace negotiations and into programmes that aim to reintegrate them into society.** Youth participation helps to build participatory democracy and helps to achieve better outcomes of disarmament, demobilization and reintegration efforts." [82] Security Council Resolution 1379 calls on states to: "Provide protection of children in peace agreements, including, where appropriate, provisions relating to the disarmament, demobilization, reintegration and rehabilitation of child soldiers and the reunification of families, and to consider, when possible, the views of children in those processes."[83]

But, with the possible exception of Sierra Leone,[84] there are no good examples of where youth have been actively involved in peace negotiations and/or transitions even though the principle of consultation with youth is quite well integrated into the work of UNICEF, most NGOs, and some aid agencies. McIntrye and Thusi note that in Sierra Leone, youth groups such as Youth for Sustainable Development (YOSUPA) and Movement of Concerned Kono Youths (MOCKY) were "credited with playing a very positive role in consolidating the peace in the area through mediation of disputes."[85] The Sierra Leone Ministry for Youth and Sport developed a "Youth Radio" and a Youth Council to provide mechanisms for youth to communicate their needs. Children and youth gave testimony to the Sierra Leone Truth and Reconciliation Commission. However, McIntyre and Thusi maintain that youth issues were not adequately addressed during the peace process and that marginalization of youth continued in the peacebuilding phase.[86] There have been questions too about the adequacy of funding for youth institutions. So, while the Sierra Leone case supports the notion that youth have an important contribution to make in peace processes, it also demonstrates that there remains a lack of official commitment to following through with sustained measures to integrate youth into politics and peacebuilding.

There are at least four reasons beyond the human rights imperative that much more emphasis should be placed on mainstreaming the participation of both children and youth into conflict negotiation, peace processes, and peacebuilding practices. First, the presence of youth in war and their contradictory absence from political decision making may help reproduce violent conflict in several ways. Second, political exclusion of youth may work against dynamics such as political involvement and leadership that promote psychological resilience.[87] Third, youth exclusion certainly results in the loss of vital knowledge about war and peace, and, fourth, it perpetuates norms of exclusion that work against values believed supportive of human rights culture and reconciliation.[88] There is the danger, then, of creating or re-creating large populations of marginalized and militarized youth that have minimal stake in peace with a peacebuilding mechanism—a new democracy, for example—that is, in itself, exclusionary. A lesson learned is that many youth feel deeply disenfranchised in postwar periods. This was true of older youth as well as adolescents; so, while lowering the voting age may be helpful, it is not the only area for attention. Yet, a number of potential benefits could accrue from more authentic involvement of youth in peace processes and political decision making thereafter, as outlined in Box 4.4.

Box 4.4: Potential Benefits of Youth Political Participation
- Brings new knowledge and ideas
- Helps transform militarized identities
- May foster psychological resilience
- May foster youth "buy in"—working against a return to violence and/or antisocial behavior
- Is a requirement of a human rights culture
- Creates a new space of youth peer interaction
- Helps transfer peace messages more broadly through social networks of youth.

Consultation with youth is different from participation in program development which is, in turn, very different from real power. Active opportunities for youth to participate in peace negotiations and post-conflict decision making at the elite level should be fostered. In some cases the competencies already exist among youth. In others they could be developed through training programs viewed as a long-term investment, not only in democracy, but also in job skills. The primary barrier exists in elites—local and international—whose mindsets would have to change. Positive first steps would entail improving communications between political elites and existing youth structures, creating new youth institutions and mechanisms to give young people access to decision making, and addressing the barriers posed by entrenched elites or elder systems through education about the relative costs and benefits of youth participation.

The different peacebuilding roles of youth must be identified and supported.
Although much emphasis has been placed on youth violence, youth also participate in a number of organized and organic peacebuilding activities. For example, it is important to document the often "untold stor[ies]" of youth soldiers. While the experience of armed conflict involves extreme physical and psychological hardship and degradation, some young soldiers "make choices that do not compromise their values excessively," finding ways to protect other young recruits from excessive brutality, for example, and providing surrogate parenting.[89] Some youth intentionally do military service, as a means to moderate oth-

ers in an armed group.[90] Can these acts be valorized and used as a peacebuilding tool without further marginalizing those who did not similarly resist? This is where storytelling and national narrative building through memory projects in youth centers and schools or university-based curriculum development projects can be used. These would allow the recovery of a history that shows nonviolent resistance as well as personal struggles to make difficult moral choices.

Although it has been noted that militarized identities are widespread in post-conflict situations, many youth shun militarism when they can, and some opt instead for active bridge-building and peacebuilding roles. Often youth emphasize the creation of new social spaces, such as actively reclaiming a public fountain as a symbol of reconciliation between divided ethnic communities;[91] lobbying for and organizing opportunities for youth development and dialogue about contentious issues;[92] or living in utopian communities.[93] Forming an even wider circle are the young people who are creative "world builders"[94] in their everyday lives, who through their peer and family interactions, resist and subvert war-supporting values. However, it is still not well understood why some young people become peacebuilders while others do not. More research is necessary on the intervening factors that shape responses to trauma and armed conflict.

Moreover, a militant stance, in itself, is not inevitably violent or destabilizing. The assertive but nonviolent activism of Otpor in Serbia, for example, which used leather dress, rock music, and quite militant symbolism (the black clenched fist) to pursue a nonviolent struggle, is a good example. During the peace process in Northern Ireland, Sinn Féin youth committed minor property damage against a British military installation as part of an organized protest and day of civil disobedience. This protest provided a focus for continued activism against the British state once armed struggle had been suspended, and was an important safety valve, perhaps, although it initially angered the party leadership.[95] It is important for policymakers who wish to promote youth peacebuilding to allow the local context, and youth themselves, to shape its terms.

A generally higher profile for youth peacebuilding work, without identifying specific programs, would raise the morale of young activists and perform a wider function in educating the public about the constructive, nonviolent roles of youth in their communities. Second, general invitations to youth to apply for reconstruction funds for the purposes of working towards peace are as important as targeting specific known and proven groups for funding. It was mentioned earlier that youth may seek integration and not reintegration. Likewise, in contexts of protracted conflicts, much so-called peacebuilding work has a "same old" quality for youth. Particularly disparaged are the perceived "hands across the barricades" or "pacification" projects that aspire to build bridges between groups where there is no real basis for living together in a new way: that is, the practical things such as violence, land, employment, trauma, the powerful symbolism and meaning of the conflict, and the political exclusion of certain groups are not being addressed.

Peacebuilding initiatives for youth could address these core issues through service-learning education, public-works projects, youth peace and reconstruction corps, and active inclusion of youth in peace negotiations and transitional justice initiatives. Another lesson is that the provocative and critical questions youth ask can lead to healing dialogue and, as basic information, are important to know if the intention is to get at the heart of what is driving conflict or making healing difficult.[96] It may be valuable to provide a variety of forums—in government offices, community meetings, classrooms, places of worship—for youth to directly ask hard questions of adults, and collaborate with them in reaching answers, whether they are questions about the past or present. It would also be useful to apply what has been learned about the value of participant symmetry in interethnic groups[97] to youth-adult collaborations, promoting authentic shared power.

Youth educate each other in complex social networks that will amplify policy mistakes and successes.
Missteps in addressing or in failing to address the practical material and safety needs, trauma and social meanings, political marginalization, peace roles and potential, and violence roles and potential of youth will be multiplied because youth educate each other. This theme has been interwoven throughout the chapter, but it bears emphasis. Perhaps more than any other social group, young people interact in a web of different social spaces. They move from home or refugee camp to school to streets and often through gangs, militia, religious organizations, workplaces, peace groups, and sports and leisure settings. These interactions have socializing effects, create support networks, shape the wider social and political context, and result in ideological reproduction and/or transformation.[98] These networks also provide ready-made routes for the transfer of peace messages.

Youth-centered reconstruction should be holistic and publicized as a peace dividend.
Youth-centered reconstruction should be holistic, planned early, implemented in full as a priority, and widely publicized as a peace dividend. Education, both in schools and informally, has an important role bridging all of the mains tasks of reconstruction. Since the factors propelling youth into armed conflict are interlocking, so must be the mechanisms used to attempt to break cycles of violence after war. A hybrid transdisciplinary peacebuilding framework aids analysis, but a more difficult question is how to translate it into a practical implementation scheme that is also holistic. For example, if one attempts to apply the lessons learned from studies of youth in conflict and post-conflict situations to a practical reconstruction tool, are the issues clarified or complicated? Figure 4.1 takes the task areas of the U.S. State Department's "Reconstruction Matrix"—security, governance and participation, humanitarian assistance and social well-being, economic stabilization and infrastructure, justice and reconciliation—and attempts to match them with lessons learned about youth issues, roles, and needs.[99]

Figure 4.1: Youth Issues, Roles, and Needs in a Reconstruction Matrix

Reconstruction Tasks	Youth Issues	Youth Roles	Youth Needs
Security	Youth as victims		Protection
	Return to violence by youth re-recruited or re-abducted	Ex-combatant transitioning	Economic inclusion
		Spoiler	Political inclusion
	Unstable peace with youth exclusion, recreational & political agitation	Criminal gang & militia member	Community defense role
		New security forces	
	New generation of recruits & new cycle of violence	New militant/ terrorist	Education (e.g., human rights)
		Peer educator	
Governance & Participation	Age of enfranchisement;	Marginal/excluded	Political inclusion
	Rate of voter participation by youth & impact of youth vote	Political spoiler	
	Other youth participation (e.g., youth councils)	Peace constituency	
	Role in negotiations & transition decision making	Peer educator/ Ideological reproduction & transformation	Education (e.g., political skills)
Humanitarian Assistance & Social Well-Being	Reunification/repatriation of displaced youth	Victim/recipient client/partner	Safety
	Physical & psychosocial health of youth	Community worker/aid worker	Economic inclusion
	Access to education of different types	Ideological reproduction & transformation	Education (e.g., basic)
Economic Stabilization & Infrastructure	Employment generation & start up Funds for youth; public works projects Youth in shadow economy Symbolism of economic opportunity	Head of household	Economic inclusion
		Driver of economy	Education (e.g., vocational)
Justice & Reconciliation	Official abuse & detention of youth	Rights bearer	Political inclusion
	Youth integrated into new police & military	New security forces	
	Prosecution for war crimes	Peer educator	Education (e.g., civic or service learning)
	Participation of youth in truth commissions, community-based healing mechanisms, national narrative building, etc.	Rights monitor	
	Human rights & peace education		

The basic breakdown of tasks is taken from Reconstruction Task Matrix, http://www.state.gov/s/crs/rls/52959.htm.

All of the main tasks of post-conflict reconstruction have important youth dimensions. This underlines the desirability of a more intentional, centered position for youth in peace processes and post-conflict reconstruction processes. The different task categories in this matrix demonstrate the necessity of utilizing the insights of all of the existing literatures—the child rights, security, development, education and psychology approaches—in addressing youth. But when youth issues, roles, and needs are applied to these reconstruction tasks, a close connection between some tasks and a number of areas of overlap and tension in dealing with youth are shown. For example, youth political roles in post-conflict situations tend to be outside official governance structures, as marginal spoiler actors (a security issue), or as an underestimated peace constituency (which has no clear place in this task matrix). Age of enfranchisement or other participation measures (governance), reintegration and rehabilitation programs (humanitarian), and jobs (economic), may all impact whether or not there is demobilization or a new generation of recruits (security).

Education in the U.S. State Department's reconstruction matrix is categorized under "humanitarian and social well-being." But, as the distribution of youth needs and roles across the different task categories shows, education measures have important roles across all categories, and in practice bridge several tasks. For example, education is also important in pursuing "justice and reconciliation" through human rights education for "security" personnel who will deal with youth, as well as through schools-based peace education, and in training programs for democratic participation and "governance." Likewise, as was noted above, economic inclusion of youth might be linked with "justice and reconciliation," not just symbolically, but also as a practical peacebuilding measure: jobs in human rights monitoring or in gathering oral histories from older citizens for the purposes of national narrative building, for example. The skills necessary for such employment would likely be delivered through schools and university-based training programs.

This tool does not allow the subtleties and complexities of youth roles or the dilemmas involved in youth issues to be clearly seen. What is clarified by this table, however, is that an approach focused on holistic needs—security, economic, political, educational, and ideological—will straddle the issue areas and that, to avoid the dilution of youth issues, key personnel involved in reconstruction efforts must have an integrated vision of the importance of youth issues to the whole of postwar reconstruction.

Certainly, this seems to be one of the key challenges that the minister for youth in Sierra Leone, Dennis Bright, has noted: "The biggest challenge is for people to listen, both locally and internationally. The second one is for people to actually accept that the youth problem is an emergency and has to be treated as such, and not as a diluted cross-cutting issue that disappears into sectoral concerns. That is the second major challenge. The third challenge is to avoid heavy bureaucratic over-conceptualisation of things."[100]

Conclusion

Few cases can be found where youth taking part in political violence were not involved for economic reasons, that is, because engagement in armed conflict helped secure basic survival needs, involved direct payments or payments to families, or was understood by the youth participant to be partly justified by a larger context of deprivation or economic inequality (not necessarily akin to their own economic status). But there seem to be few cases where economic reasons entirely explain participation. A development approach to youth in post-conflict situations is vitally necessary but not sufficient to address the complex challenges youth pose. Yet, the other prevailing approaches, child rights and security, seem to pull at opposite ends of the problem with youth uncomfortably caught in between. Post-conflict education is well recognized as a peacebuilding tool. But if education is conceptualized as belonging to a particular policy sector, then the contributions education and training programs can make to such areas as policing, governance, and transitional justice may be underappreciated. Finally, memory and trauma, and the stories, sacred and secular, that young people tell about themselves, their communities, and their enemies, construct a foundation for more war but can also be a fount of peace.

The multidimensional challenge of youth and postwar reconstruction has informed these conclusions:

1. *Every context is different.* Youth strategies in post-conflict situations should begin with a comprehensive, transdisciplinary assessment of the impact of the conflict on youth, and of youth on the conflict. Closing the gap between child rights advocacy and security analysis is a role for scholars and practitioners in the field of conflict management and peacebuilding. Close consultation with local experts and especially with youth themselves is essential.

2. *All of the main tasks of postwar reconstruction have important youth dimensions.* Key personnel involved in reconstruction efforts must have an integrated vision of the importance of youth issues to the whole of postwar reconstruction. An important role exists for youth advisors on the ground in helping to bridge crosscutting youth concerns and to minimize dilution of youth issues.

3. *Design with youth in mind.* To have confidence in a better future, youth must perceive that economic opportunities await them and that they have been included in measures to acknowledge and rectify crimes of the past. Economic revitalization measures and transitional justice mechanisms should be designed with youth participation and youth roles, issues, and needs clearly in mind, and with youth policy advisors on the ground to advocate for the continuing involvement of youth.

4. *Economic initiatives and transitional justice will not be enough.* Ceding some significant political power to youth requires a mindset change at all levels, from local to international political elites, and among youth themselves. Further education about the relative costs and benefits of youth political participation is needed along with serious efforts to include children and youth in peace negotiations and post-conflict decision making.

5. *Education can be a bridge.* An intervening/interim policy is to focus on education (in both formal and informal settings) in ways that serve not only economic futures but the needs and abilities of youth to be actively involved in ideological reproduction and/or transformation, national narrative building, and community service. These are the other strong motives—along with economic ones—for involvement in armed conflict.

6. *Security in post-conflict situations will be threatened by youth in a variety of ways.* The most effective responses will be ones that make redemptive violence less attractive, and that address needs for economic security and participation. The dilemmas involved in protecting while also confronting children and youth in armed conflict should be more publicly acknowledged, along with an intentional and public strategy of maintaining a human rights-based approach to youth combatants (especially those under eighteen).

7. *Make peacebuilding projects directly relevant to young people's lives and aspirations.* Peacebuilding projects for youth should address the "hard" issues, such as violence on the streets, economic needs, and political exclusion, through mechanisms such as service-learning education, public works projects, and youth peace and reconstruction corps. There is also a need for further research on the reasons why some youth choose to be agents of peace rather than agents of violence.

8. *Youth-centered reconstruction should be holistic.* It will mean forging a difficult balance between the entrenched interests of elders and/or elites, and youth desires for new structures and approaches. Youth consultations and local community mediations should precede interventions and continue along with, and after, project implementation.

9. *Tangible gains for youth are a litmus test for the legitimacy and sustainability of a peace or transition process.* Youth-centered reconstruction should be planned early, implemented in full and as a priority, and widely publicized as a peace dividend.

In the end, the challenge is to really listen. Many post-conflict projects involve consultation with youth. Often such participation is enshrined as a key principle following the Convention on the Rights of the Child, and almost all analyses (including this one) contain the obligatory quotations or testimony from youth. But adults need to be more reflective about how they process this information, how to recognize the biases and vested interests they bring to that analysis, and how closely what they conclude conforms to the real needs and wishes of youth. Again, this is where a transdisciplinary methodology may be useful, for different academic disciplines and professional bureaucracies pursue and process these answers differently. Sustained and careful listening to youth representatives and youth as a whole, through a variety of means, including surveys, ethnography, and open forums, is essential, if youth are not to be trapped in silence in postwar situations. If they *are* trapped in silence, and remain caught between the concerns of child rights activists and security analysts, the chances of breaking the cycles of violence in contemporary wars will be bleak.

AFTERWORD
What Do We Know About Peacebuilding?
Eileen F. Babbitt

The excellent essays in this volume, condensed versions of three much longer edited works, provide an opportunity to review what we know about peacebuilding. Although the practice of trying to put states back together after war has spanned many decades, the scholarship of what constitutes effective peacebuilding is much more recent, spurred by the enormous challenge of Bosnia in 1995 and extending to Iraq in 2006. What have we learned from these experiences that will be useful in the future?

Early analytic efforts (i.e., 1994–96) focused on the importance of international engagement in the implementation of a peace agreement, especially if that agreement had been mediated. Research showed that the parties in conflict were very often unable to carry out implementation on their own without continuing oversight and assistance, calling for an ongoing commitment from international actors to make the peacebuilding efforts succeed.[1]

And what were these international actors supposed to do? Another strand of research created a catalog or typology of tasks to be done.[2] The daunting list included internal and external security; judicial reform and rule of law; constitution making and revamping governance structures; rebuilding the economy and financial institutions; the return of refugees and internally displaced persons (IDPs); and developing a functioning civil society. In Bosnia, for example, these tasks were all tackled simultaneously, with various specialized intergovernmental and nongovernmental organizations taking the lead in each sector. The coordination was supposedly to happen through the office of a designated "high representative," a position created by the Dayton Accords. The results were initially faltering at best, improving as the international actors gained more experience. We began to understand the need for

---

Eileen Babbitt is professor of International Conflict Management Practice and director of the International Negotiation and Conflict Resolution Program at the Fletcher School of Law and Diplomacy, Tufts University.

ongoing international commitment and a sense of what should be on the list of things to do, but how to accomplish these overwhelming tasks effectively was not yet known.

The next phase of scholarship, published from 1997–2002, tackled this question and came up with recommendations on sequencing.[3] The consensus seemed to be that internal security was the most important prerequisite for peacebuilding. Unless physical security could be reasonably well guaranteed, all other tasks were more difficult, even impossible, to achieve. Unfortunately, as the ongoing struggles in Afghanistan and Iraq demonstrate, that lesson has not yet been learned by those who plan and implement peacebuilding operations.[4]

In parallel to the sequencing discussion, scholars and practitioners were documenting real-world case studies to report what was actually happening on the ground in various peacebuilding operations. Thus we started collecting more detail about specific tasks, trying to find successful models that could be tried and built upon elsewhere.[5] In addition, comparative analyses across differing cases allowed us to push the boundaries on specific topics, asking new questions that hadn't been foreseen until enough data were available to illuminate them.[6]

Contributions of the RIREC Series

The three volumes edited by Borer, Darby, and McEvoy-Levy—with the major findings of each summarized in this small volume—are a welcome addition to this evolving literature. Besides providing excellent summaries of the work to date on two of the significant issues already on the "list" of peacebuilding activities—security and transitional justice—they refine the developing conventional wisdom in these arenas as well as draw our attention to the often-forgotten needs of young people caught up in mass violence.

I'd like to highlight a few of their findings that I think are particularly noteworthy.

On violence:
- Violence is not only perpetrated by insurgent groups, but also by *governments.* This is a very important point that has not received enough attention in the rush to punish violence by "terrorists," who are by definition always drawn from groups outside government circles. Government-sponsored violence can be especially problematic when the government is dominated by one identity group; this leaves other identity groups, often numerical as well as political minorities, to continue harboring distrust of the new post-settlement structures being built. Amazingly, this can happen even when the international community has complete power during a transition. Kosovo is a prime example.

- Violence by nongovernmental groups has multiple motivations, but one is the uncertainty of government follow-through on promises made during the peace negotiations to downsize or change the composition of security forces. As Allison Hodgkins of the Fletcher School of Law and Diplomacy at Tufts University argues, peace negotiations in intra-state identity conflicts are conducted as if the two contending parties are symmetrical in their capacity to follow through on the elements of peace agreements. In fact, they are not. The most significant example is that governments are not expected to disarm whereas insurgent groups are. This is inherently asymmetrical, and creates very big implementation problems for the insurgent group. To date, this asymmetry has not been recognized by the international community, which often then blames the insurgent group for its inability to enforce the deal.[7]

- The police are a crucial player in post-settlement security. Chapter 2 refers to them as "reluctant reformers," and that conforms to my experience in the Balkans region as well. This is one of the first institutions that must function well, to keep civil order in the volatile transition period. In addition, the police are expected to perform in accordance with democratic principles, even before vetting, recruiting, and training of new officers takes place. It is an impossible and thankless task. They are seen as either captives of a biased national regime or tools of international imperialists, and in either case therefore untrustworthy. In Iraq, for example, they have consistently been the target of suicide bombings and other violent attacks.

In my view, the police are one of the key barometers of progress in the peacebuilding agenda. They are the most visible daily interface between the government and the population, and therefore a window into the level of working trust in that relationship. It requires not only focusing on the right composition, mandate, and training; it also requires the change from a perception—on the part of both the public and the police themselves—that the police are oppressors to their being seen as servants of the society. If the government and the international community can get police reform right, it is the key to providing both physical and psychological security.

On transitional justice:
- Each new peace process brings a slightly altered mode of truth seeking, which is really as it should be; context matters in terms of finding a design that suits the circumstances. However, some of the trends are problematic. For example, the time and money spent on international tribunals has led to unrealistic restrictions on subsequent so-called hybrid tribunals, which compromise their ultimate effectiveness. Trials

are, by nature, expensive and time-consuming processes; that is why alternative dispute resolution has become so popular in the United States! However, since one of the reasons for using prosecutions in truth seeking is to educate the public about the rule of law, the quality of these trials should not be compromised. If done badly, these tribunals will confirm any suspicion lurking in the public's mind about the efficacy of the rule of law, setting back the peacebuilding agenda considerably.

In my experiences in the Balkans, people have very high expectations about the role that prosecutions can play in reforming their societies. Of all the approaches to transitional justice, prosecutions are the most favored by a wide margin. When I talked with people there about why that is true, the response was twofold: to demonstrate that there are institutions acting impartially to protect the rights of all citizens, including minorities; and to show that no one in the society, including high-ranking officials and military officers, are beyond the reach of the law. This is crucial to restructuring the social contract in these societies, and it therefore must be done with the utmost care. Cutting corners in putting together tribunals may create short-term savings but can be a long-term mistake.

- Scholars and practitioners are just beginning to ask whether these truth-seeking processes have the intended impact on society. To date, we have collectively asserted their importance, but there has been little study to see if in fact that is true. As Chapter 3 rightly notes, measuring impact is very challenging. What are we to measure-truth, justice, reconciliation, closure, healing, national unity? When are we to measure it? And how much progress on any of these elements signals success?

Evaluation is problematic for peacebuilding in general. An interesting literature is now developing on this issue, drawing tools from international development[8] as well as from psychology, adult learning theory, institutional change theory, and many other disciplines. What is emerging from this literature is that good evaluation begins with a clear definition of what you are trying to change; an articulated theory of how the change might take place; and a well-designed set of implementable steps that correspond with that theory. In addition, good evaluation does not take place just at the end of a program; it should be integrated into a program from its inception, in order to provide feedback and learning along the way so that adjustments may be made. [9]

Drawing again from my experience in the Balkans, I believe that transitional justice programs are not sufficiently plugged into this evaluation trend. Because of their sensitive content, they are often fighting difficult political battles to gain both government and public support, and using primarily moral rhetoric to argue their case.[10] We need more systematic collection of data on these efforts, in order to provide advocates with the analytic tools they need to show how truth seeking can provide short- and long-term benefits, and to make sure that such programs are designed in the best ways possible. Most truth-seeking efforts fail to include evaluation as an integral component, and that may be an easy correction to make that could move us in the right direction.

On youth:

- More than any other demographic group in conflict zones, youth are both victims and perpetrators. It is therefore critical to take them specifically into account in peacebuilding efforts, as data discussed in Chapter 4 show that the presence of the so-called "youth bulge" of young males is a big risk factor leading to civil wars.

   However, the data also show that young people can be peacemakers, and to assume they are *only* perpetrators or victims runs another risk—of discounting what they can bring to the peacebuilding effort. For example, in Serbia and Kosovo, two of the most well-known and well-respected NGOs working on transitional justice issues are the Youth Initiative on Human Rights in Belgrade, and the Kosovo Research and Documentation Institute (KODI) in Pristina. This is quite significant in a region where many of the young people are leaving because they see no hope for their future, or are apathetic because they see no improvement in the social or political conditions in which they live. In Bosnia, for example, youth (defined as ages fourteen to twenty-nine) make up 23 percent of the population. In a 2005 survey done there, 45–60 percent of this age group were unemployed, and 77 percent say they want to leave Bosnia. The greatest complaint is with the educational system, but unemployment, lack of hope for the future, and political instability are also cited as reasons to leave. Over 120,000 have already left the state since the war.[11]

   Thus, like police reform, retaining youth *in constructive political and economic roles* can be another measurable assessment for the impact of peacebuilding efforts.

- The notion of framing youth-centered reconstruction as a "peace dividend" is a brilliant idea. In every conflict-ridden country, the primary concern of adults is for the well-being of their children. Often they will say, "We may not be able to change the country for ourselves, but we want to make things better for our children, so they don't suffer as we have." If adults, including government leaders, can see *tangible* benefits accruing to their children from their decisions to pursue peace, implementation of peace agreements may be enhanced.

This means not only the obvious focus on job creation and skills training for young people, but also on building an education system that truly prepares them to be successful in the world. The challenge, of course, is that education is more of a long-term investment, with results not necessarily seen immediately. However, innovative curriculum development and the rebuilding of schools are the short-term steps that could lead to enticing young people to stay—resulting in measurable impacts as I've noted above.

- The analysis in Chapter 4 demonstrates the importance of interdisciplinary research to inform peacebuilding efforts. Because peacebuilding itself is a complex enterprise, the analysis that supports it will be much more relevant if it reflects that complexity. By drawing on the literature of human rights, security studies, psychology, international development, and education, we are able to see the myriad ways in which peacebuilding and youth are related. Each by itself gives us only a sliver of truth; but like the story of the blind men and the elephant, each truth by itself is incomplete.

  For example, if "youth" are only seen as the young males in the "youth bulge" who pose a potential threat to peace and security, the resulting policy prescription will completely miss the important dimensions of youth as peacemakers, family members, and members of an increasingly interlinked intercommunal and global youth network. In fact, as the next section shows, a holistic view goes beyond any one issue, and allows us to see the linkages across issues as well.

On the linkages between security, truth seeking, and youth:
- In looking at violence, it is crucial to recognize that in most violent conflicts the fighters are drawn primarily from the youth of the country. In some cases, even children are conscripted. Therefore violence prevention and mitigation must take into account the very insightful analysis presented here of the special needs of youth so these are not overlooked. For example, demobilization, disarmament, and reintegration (DDR) programs that might work for adults might miss the psychological and developmental components that are needed to be effective with young soldiers.
- Truth-seeking processes must reach out specifically to groups in the population whose needs are often ignored: women and young people. As I have found in my work on transitional justice in the Balkans, all people in a region affected by war must be included in truth seeking in order for it to have the intended results: strengthening the rule of law, preventing manipulation of the past by ruthless leaders, and contributing to the process of reconciliation.[12] If important groups are left out, the truth will not be complete, many psychological wounds will remain—and the society as a whole will suffer the consequences.

- Finally, truth seeking is a very important component of security. People from a war zone who see their government covering up or manipulating past events or who feel that their experiences in war have not been acknowledged or validated, can not feel secure with those who govern them. There will always be the fear that they can be at risk again, with no warning, because those who perpetrated such crimes in the past have not been identified or held accountable. Therefore, not only for the purposes of justice and reconciliation, but also for the purpose of establishing psychological and even physical security, truth seeking is a crucial task.

Where Do We Go from Here?

As with all excellent research, this series of edited volumes has both enhanced our understanding and illuminated a new set of questions. Our understanding of this very complex process we refer to as peacebuilding is increasing, step by step, but I think we'd all agree that there is still a long way to go before we can truly say we know how to do this well. I'd like to highlight two issues that should be next on the research agenda.

First is the need to provide more explicit guidance to the peacemakers, those who negotiate peace agreements, in how to avoid the pitfalls they may be unwittingly setting up for peacebuilding. As Christine Bell astutely noted, peace agreements ". . . are best thought of as distinctively transitional constitutions," which ". . . set out the organs of government and the other institutions of the society, and the nature of the relationship between the individual and the state."[13] The essays in this volume clearly illustrate Bell's point: everything from DDR, police reform, and civilian control of the military, to prosecutions of war criminals and stipulations for education reform are set out in peace agreements. All future agreements should therefore draw heavily upon the accumulating wisdom about implementation, so that the content of agreements enable rather than inhibit constructive change. At present, there is no international institution whose responsibility it is to keep track of lessons learned, so each negotiation process begins almost from scratch.

Another crucial aspect of peace negotiations is the decision about who should be at the table, in order that peacebuilding processes respond to the needs of all segments of society. For example, UN Security Council Resolution 1325, passed in October 2000, "...*Urges* Member States to ensure increased representation of women at all decision-making levels in national, regional and international institutions and mechanisms for the prevention, management, and resolution of conflict."[14] Many women's organizations have interpreted this to include women's representation in bodies negotiating peace agreements. However, the resolution has yet to have a big impact on women's inclusion in this all-male reserve. No resolution yet exists to address youth's inclusion.

A second issue that requires more research is how to accomplish the short-term tasks in ways that support positive long-term development. For example, how does a state in transition create internal security in the short term while at the same time laying the groundwork for building a police force and judicial system that will be trusted by all of the population? In Kosovo, for example, internal security has been handled by the NATO Kosovo Force (KFOR) since the cessation of fighting in 1999. However, even with the presence of international troops, many Serbs have left Kosovo out of fear for their safety. In 2004, a surge of Albanian violence toward Serbs led many more to have grave doubts about the ability of internationals to protect them. As of summer 2006, seven years after the de facto separation of Kosovo from Serbia, the Kosovo Police Service (KPS) is still subservient to UNMIK (the civilian authority in Kosovo), and Kosovo Serbs do not feel safe outside of their own enclaves. In the likelihood of Kosovo independence from Serbia, the groundwork for a system trusted by the public to mitigate violence and provide security has not been laid.

More broadly, we need to be more realistic about the time line for the rebuilding of a country after war, especially to establish it as a functioning liberal democracy. More often than not, the international community sets benchmarks based upon their own political needs. An example was the decision to hold municipal elections in Bosnia only one year after the Dayton Accords were signed so that the U.S. government could promise its electorate that U.S. troops would only be committed that long (which turned out to be an empty promise). In fact, history teaches us that democracy building was a centuries-long process in Europe, and even in the United States. It is unrealistic to expect that countries recovering from mass violence will be able to accomplish this in a few short years. We must determine more realistic benchmarks for progress and a more supportive role for international actors to play over time, not only as overseers but as coaches and mentors.

The learning curve on peacebuilding over the last seventeen years, since the end of the Cold War, has been a steep one. Lessons learned have not necessarily been lessons applied. We must keep asking the hard questions, as these scholars have done, so that the learning process continues.

Notes

CHAPTER 1

1. Harbom and Wallensteen, "Armed Conflict and Its International Dimensions." For more detailed data, see the Uppsala Conflict Data Project, http://www.pcr.uu.se/database/index.php.

2. Comprehensive Peace Agreements (CPAs) are distinguished from the hundreds of partial peace agreements signed during this period by setting out to address all the issues in dispute, as defined by the major negotiators.

3. The Kroc Institute for International Peace Studies at the University of Notre Dame hosts the Peace Matrix Project, which sets out to compare recent and current peace agreements.

4. Uppsala Conflict Data Project Web site, http://www.pcr.uu.se/research/UCDP/UCDP_toplevel.htm.

5. United States Institute of Peace, Peace Agreements Digital Collection: http://www.usip.org/library/pa.html.

6. Richmond, *Transformation of Peace*, 6.

7. Among many examples see Peters, *Pathways to Peace*, and Cox, Guelke, and Stephen, *A Farewell to Arms?*

8. See, as examples, Sisk, *Democratization in South Africa*, and du Toit, *South Africa's Brittle Peace.*

9. Doyle, Johnstone, and Orr, *Keeping the Peace.*

10. Hampson, *Nurturing Peace.*

11. Darby and Mac Ginty, *Management of Peace Processes;* Darby and Mac Ginty, *Contemporary Peacemaking.*

12. Gurr, *Minorities at Risk.*

13. Geller and Singer, *Nations at War.*

14. Harbom and Wallensteen, "Armed Conflict and Its International Dimensions."

15. PIOOM Databank, *PIOOM World Conflict Map.*

16. Zartman, *Ripe for Resolution.*

17. Haass, *Conflicts Unending.*

18. Wallensteen and Sollenberg, "Armed Conflict 1989–2000."

19. Licklider, "The Consequences of Negotiated Settlements."

20. Hartzell, Hoddie, and Rothchild, "Stabilizing the Peace."

21. See, for example, Call and Stanley, "Military and Police Reform."

22. Doyle, Johnstone and Orr, *Keeping the Peace.*

23. See, for example, Stedman, Rothchild, and Cousens, *Ending Civil Wars.*

24. Bartkus, *The Dynamic of Secession.*

25. Mac Ginty, *No War, No Peace.*

26. Collier and Hoeffler, "Greed and Grievance."

27. Arnson and Zartman, *Rethinking the Economics of War.*

28. Kroc Institute, "The Horizon of Peacebuilding."

29. McEvoy-Levy, ed., *Troublemakers or Peacemakers?*

30. Kemper, *Youth in War-to-Peace Transitions.*

31. Urdal, "The Devil in the Demographics"; Cincotta, "Youth Bulge, Underemployment."

32. See Brett and McCallin, *Invisible Soldiers;* Brett and Sprecht, *Young Soldiers;* 2004; Singer, *Children at War.*

33. See, for example, Boyden and de Berry, *Children and Youth.*

34. For an excellent review of the effects of post-accord crime, see Mac Ginty, "Post-Accord Crime."

35. See Darby, ed., *Violence and Reconstruction.*

36. See McEvoy-Levy, ed., *Troublemakers or Peacemakers?* and chapter 4 in this volume.

37. Hayner, *Unspeakable Truths;* C. Bell, *Peace Agreements;* Borer, ed., *Telling the Truths.*

38. Tristan Anne Borer, ed., *Telling the Truths: Truth Telling and Peace Building in Post-Conflict Societies;* John Darby, ed., *Violence and Reconstruction;* and Siobhán McEvoy-Levy, ed., *Troublemakers or Peacemakers? Youth and Post-Accord Peace Building* (all published by University of Notre Dame Press, 2006).

39. Stedman, Rothchild, and Cousens, *Ending Civil Wars;* Kriesberg, *Constructive Conflicts.*

40. See Cox, Guelke, and Stephen, *A Farewell to Arms?*

41. See Hermann and Newman, "Path Strewn with Thorns."

42. See, as examples, Morkel, "Peace Dividends," and du Toit, "Why Post-Settlement Settlements."

43. See Stedman, Rothchild, and Cousens, *Ending Civil Wars.*

44. See Hermann and Newman, "Path Strewn with Thorns."

45. This debate did not include those who argued against any sort of dealing with the past, and who favored a policy of letting "bygones be bygones." In contrast, the literature noted here deals specifically with those who favored transitional justice, but who differed on the appropriate mechanism for delivering it.

46. Rotberg and Thompson, eds., *Truth v. Justice.*

47. Aspen Institute, *State Crimes.*

48. See chapter 3 in this volume, and Perriello and Wierda, *Special Court for Sierra Leone.*

49. See McEvoy-Levy, ed., *Troublemakers or Peacemakers?* and chapter 4 in this volume.

50. Richmond, *Transformation of Peace.*

51. Mac Ginty, *No War, No Peace.*

52. Jeong, *Peacebuilding in Postconflict Societies,* 15.

CHAPTER 2

1. Darby, ed., *Violence and Reconstruction.*
2. McEvoy-Levy, ed., *Troublemakers or Peacemakers?*
3. Stedman, "Spoiler Problems in Peace Processes," 95.
4. Stedman, Rothchild, and Cousens, *Ending Civil Wars.*
5. See, for example, chapters by Stedman and Zahar in Darby and Mac Ginty, eds., *Contemporary Peacemaking.*
6. Borer, ed., *Telling the Truths.*
7. Gamba, "Post-Agreement Demobilization, Disarmament, and Reconstruction."
8. Mac Ginty, "Biting the Bullet," 238.
9. See, for example, Call and Stanley, "Military and Police Reform."
10. Höglund and Zartman, "Violence and the State," 14.
11. Darby, *The Effects of Violence on Peace Processes.*
12. The Economist, "Uneasy Peace."
13. Official crime statistics are published by police services in South Africa and Northern Ireland. The statistics in the following paragraphs, and in Graphs 1 and 2, are taken from these published statistics. The South African Police Service publishes *Crime Statistics* annually. *Crime Statistics for Northern Ireland* is also updated regularly by the Police Service of Northern Ireland.
14. Reed, "Mbeki Confident as Serious Crime Falls."
15. Mac Ginty, "Post-Accord Crime," 117.
16. *The Economist,* "Uneasy Peace."
17. Du Toit, "Why Post-Settlement Settlements?"
18. Gamba, "Post-Agreement Demobilization, Disarmament, and Reconstruction," 54.
19. Ibid., 66.
20. Murray, "Post-Accord Police Reform," 98.
21. Ibid., 100.
22. Sisk, "Political Violence after Peace Talks," 137.
23. Zahar, "Spoilers in Peace Processes," 40.
24. Sisk, "Political Violence after Peace Talks," 125.
25. Höglund and Zartman, "Violence and the State," 18.
26. Zahar, "Spoilers in Peace Processes," 34.
27. Sisk, "Political Violence after Peace Talks," 128.
28. Ibid., 133.
29. Darby and Mac Ginty, *Contemporary Peacemaking,* 245–55.
30. Du Toit, *South Africa's Brittle Peace,* 16–60.
31. Rohter, "Like Carrot, Stick Fails with Rebels in Colombia."
32. Sisk, "Political Violence after Peace Talks," 131.

CHAPTER 3

1. Kurtenbach, "Dealing with the Past," 356.

2. Huyse, "Dealing with the Past," 327.

3. While studies of accountability for crimes committed during the Holocaust raise similar questions, they are not generally considered part of the literature on transitional justice — the general reference to "transitions" being initially to the Latin American transitions and thereafter to post-Cold War transitions to democracy. Questions about accounting for gross human rights violations committed during the Holocaust are generally considered under the rubric of "Holocaust studies."

4. Borer, "Truth Telling as a Peace-Building Activity," 17.

5. Freeman, "Essentials of Transitional Justice."

6. Inter-American Court on Human Rights, Velásquez Rodríguez case.

7. Méndez, "The Human Right to Truth."

8. International Center for Transitional Justice, *Annual Report*.

9. Hybrid tribunals, the newest generation of international criminal tribunals, are staffed by a combination of both national and international judges, prosecutors, and defense attorneys.

10. Borer, "Truth Commissions," 338–40.

11. Hayner, *Unspeakable Truths*, 14–17.

12. For detailed information on these commissions, see either the United States Institute of Peace's Truth Commissions Digital Collection (http://www.usip.org/library/truth.html), or the International Center for Transitional Justice Web site (http://www.ictj.org/en/index.html).

13. International Center for Transitional Justice, *Annual Report*, 23.

14. See the chapters in Borer, ed., *Telling the Truths*.

15. While there is general consensus on the need to deal with the past in order to achieve sustainable peace, not all scholars agree. Andrew Rigby notes that "one could argue that you can have too much memory. Too great a concern with remembering the past can mean that the divisions and conflicts of old never die, the wounds are never healed" (Rigby, *Justice and Reconciliation*, 2). Moreover, there are cases in which societies have consciously chosen not to engage in official truth telling — what Rigby calls "an exercise in collective amnesia" — a choice that does not appear to result in revenge or recriminations or continued divisions. The two cases of successful "collective amnesia" usually cited are post-Franco Spain and post-1994 Mozambique. For a case study of Spain, see Rigby, *Justice and Reconciliation*, 39–61. For an overview of Mozambique, see Hayner, *Unspeakable Truths*, chapter 12.

16. Mendeloff, "Truth-Seeking, Truth-Telling," 355.

17. Shaw, "Rethinking Truth and Reconciliation Commissions," 1.

18. Ibid.

19. Sierra Leone Truth and Reconciliation Commission Act.

20. Sooka, "Building Peace through Accountability," 11.

21. Méndez, "The Human Right to Truth," 133.

22. Ibid., 137–38.

23. Freeman, "The Essentials of Transitional Justice."

24. Crane, "Dancing with the Devil," 5.

25. The narrowly defined mandate (to try only those "who bear the greatest responsi-bility" for violations), a demand of the international community determined to hold down the costs associated with criminal tribunals, was a bitter pill for many citizens to swallow. Dougherty argues that "in this instance, international preferences trumped local expecta-tions that justice included prosecuting secondary perpetrators" ("Pursuing Justice on a Shoestring," 5).

26. Ibid.

27. Ibid., 13.

28. For a much more in-depth discussion of the SCSL's financial woes, see Dougherty, "Pursuing Justice on a Shoestring."

29. Leebaw, "New Approaches to Transitional Justice."

30. Boraine, "Transitional Justice as an Emerging Field."

31. Louis Bickford, personal correspondence with Tristan Anne Borer, February 27, 2006.

32. Greensboro Truth and Reconciliation Commission. Available online: http://www.greensborotrc.org/.

33. International Center for Transitional Justice, *Annual Report*, 10.

34. Garton Ash, "True Confessions," 36.

35. Cited in McEvoy-Levy, "Introduction."

36. Baxter, "Empirical Research Methodologies," 8.

37. Brahm, "Getting to the Bottom of Truth," 22.

38. Mendeloff, "Truth-Seeking, Truth-Telling."

39. Borer, "Truth Telling as a Peace-Building Activity."

40. Baxter, "Empirical Research Methodologies."

41. Human Rights Watch, *Human Rights Watch Global Report.*

42. *Truth and Reconciliation Commission of South Africa Report*, vol. 4, 296.

43. Goldblatt and Meintjes, "South African Women Demand the Truth."

44. F. Ross, *Bearing Witness*, 158.

45. Sooka, "Building Peace through Accountability," 9.

46. *Truth and Reconciliation Commission of South Africa Report*, vol. 1, 64.

47. F. Ross, *Bearing Witness*, 162.

48. Brahm, "Getting to the Bottom of Truth."

49. Hayner, "International Guidelines," 175.

50. Louis Bickford, personal correspondence with Tristan Anne Borer, February 27, 2006.

51. Freeman, "The Essentials of Transitional Justice."

52. Ibid.

CHAPTER 4

1. McIntyre, "Rights, Roots Causes and Recruitment," 11.

2. United Nations Population Division, *World Population Prospects*.

3. Ibid.

4. Ibid. In the Occupied Territories, over 50 percent of the population is under fifteen.

5. Ibid.

6. Ibid.

7. Ibid.

8. Northern Ireland Statistics and Research Agency, *Annual Abstract of Statistics*; United Nations Population Division, *World Population Prospects*.

9. Sommers, "Fearing Africa's Young Men," 2.

10. McEvoy-Levy, ed., *Troublemakers or Peacemakers?*

11. McEvoy-Levy, "Introduction."

12. Sommers, "Fearing Africa's Young Men"; Sommers, "In the Shadow of Genocide."

13. Adwan and Bar-On, "Sharing History."

14. Namik Kirlic quoted in Helsing, "Education, Sustainable Peace and Reconciliation."

15. Cilliers, "Transforming Post-Accord Education Systems"; Kirlic in Helsing, "Education, Sustainable Peace and Reconciliation."

16. Cohn and Goodwin-Gill, *Child Soldiers*; Kalshoven, "Child Soldiers"; Bracken, "Rehabilitation of Child Soldiers"; Brett and McCallin, *Children: The Invisible Soldiers*; Dennis, "Newly Adopted Protocols"; Maslen and Islamshah, "Revolution Not Evolution"; Høiskar, "Underage and Under Fire"; Keairns, *Voices of Girl Child Soldiers*; Somasundaram, "Child Soldiers"; Apfel and Simon, *Minefields in the Hearts*; Cairns, *Children and Political Violence*; and Garbarino and Kostelny, "What Children Can Tell Us." Also bringing the issue to a wider audience and linking the problems of child soldiers, child refugees, and war-affected children to wider global conflict dynamics and factors such as small arms are Boothby and Knudsen, "Children of the Gun," and Klare, "Kalashnikov Age."

17. This includes important volumes of research conducted by both scholars and by practitioners working for NGOs such as Save the Children, Christian Children's Fund, Quaker UN Office, and UNICEF, as well as research published in legal and medical journals. Graça Machel's report published by UNICEF in 1996 *(Impact of Armed Conflict on Children)* drew significant attention to the issue of war-affected children more generally. And a sizable body of advocacy literature from UNICEF, Human Rights Watch, Amnesty International, International Coalition to Stop the Use of Child Soldiers, War Child CA/International, and others provided both new knowledge about child soldiers and suggested strategies for addressing their use.

18. Machel, *Impact of Armed Conflict on Children*; and Carpenter, ed., Born of War.

19. Studies of South Africa include Straker, et al., *Faces in the Revolution;* Dawes and Donald, eds., *Children and Adversity;* Dissel, "Youth, Street Gangs and Violence"; and Marks, *Young Warriors.* Studies of Northern Ireland include Harbinson and Harbinson, Society under Stress; D. Bell, *Acts of Union;* Byrne, *Growing Up in a Divided Society;* Smyth, *Half the Battle;* Smyth et al., *Impact of Political Conflict;* Cairns, *Caught in the Crossfire;* Cairns, *Children and Political Violence;* Cairns et al., "Impact of the Peace Process in Northern Ireland"; McEvoy-Levy, "Communities and Peace"; McEvoy-Levy, "Youth, Violence and Conflict Transformation"; McEvoy-Levy, "Politics, Protest and Local 'Power-Sharing'"; and Jarman, *Managing Disorder.* Studies of Sierra Leone include Richards, *Fighting for the Rain Forest;* Zack-Williams, "Child Soldiers"; and Wessells and Jonah, "Recruitment and Reintegration." Studies of other countries include Sommers, *Fear in Bongoland* (on Tanzania); Yamani, *Changed Identities* (on Saudi Arabia); Cameron, "The Role of Children as Peace-Makers in Colombia," and Sanford, "Moral Imagination of Survival" (on Colombia); Sanford, *Buried Secrets,* and Sanford, "Moral Imagination of Survival" (on Guatemala); Thompson, "Beyond Civil Society" (on Mozambique); Barber, "Political Violence, Family Relations, and Palestinian Youth Functioning," Hart, "Beyond Struggle and Aid," and Adwan and Bar-On, "Sharing History" (on the Palestinians); Heppner, *"My Gun Was as Tall as Me"* (on Burma); Sommers, "Fearing Africa's Young Men," and "In the Shadow of Genocide" (on Rwanda); Eyber and Ager, "Researching Young Peoples' Experiences of War," and Nordstrom, "Jagged Edge of Peace" (on Angola); Mawson, "Children, Impunity and Justice" (on Uganda); Swaine and Feeny, "Neglected Perspective" (on Kosovo); and Cilliers, "Transforming Post-Accord Education Systems" (on Bosnia).

20. Brett and Sprecht, *Young Soldiers.*

21. Boyden and de Berry, *Children and Youth;* McEvoy-Levy, ed., *Troublemakers or Peacemakers?*

22. See United Nations Secretary General, *Children and Armed Conflict.* This report names fifty-four groups in eleven countries that currently recruit or use child soldiers.

23. United Nations Security Council, "Security Council Establishes Monitoring, Reporting Mechanism."

24. Bender and Frosch, "Children's Reactions to the War"; Gillespie and Allport, *Youth's Outlook on the Future;* Tolley, *Children and War;* and Ziv, Kruglanski, and Schulman, "Children's Psychological Reactions to Wartime Stress."

25. See, for example, Braungart and Braungart, "Black and White South African University Students' Perceptions"; Hakvoort, "Children's Conceptions of Peace and War"; Hakvoort and Oppenheimer, "Children and Adolescents' Conceptions"; Raviv, Oppenheimer, and Bar-Tal, *How Children Understand War and Peace;* Hall, "How Children Think and Feel about War and Peace"; Jagodic, "Is War a Good or a Bad Thing?"; L. Jones, "Adolescent Understandings of Political Violence"; Maoz, "Multiple Conflicts and Competing Agendas"; McLernon, Ferguson, and Cairns, "Comparison of Northern Irish Children's Attitudes"; Punamaki, *Childhood under Conflict;* and Speilmann, "If Peace Comes . . . ." There are multiple relevant works by these authors; the quite large psychology literature is reviewed in detail in Cairns, *Children and Political Violence.*

26. Connolly and McGinn, *Sectarianism, Children and Community Relations.*

27. Arafat with Boothby, "Psycho-Social Assessment of Palestinian Children."

28. Much of this literature focuses on Israel and the Palestinians, Northern Ireland, and South Africa. A lot more is known about how children take part in or suffer from armed conflict and how they think about and cope with war than about how their ideas about war and especially about peace develop.

29. See Cincotta, "Youth Bulge, Underemployment"; Cincotta, Engelman, and Anastasion, *Security Demographic.* For a good discussion of the different elements of the debate youth bulge theories have instigated and some of the consequences, see Kemper, *Youth in War-to-Peace Transitions.*

30. Borchini, Lanz, and O'Connell, "Child Soldiers."

31. See Singer, *Children at War.*

32. Cincotta, "Youth Bulge, Underemployment," 1.

33. See Sommers, "Fearing Africa's Young Men," for this and a further critique of youth bulge theories as they are applied to Africa; see also Urdal, "The Devil in the Demographics."

34. Sommers, "Fearing Africa's Young Men," cites specific examples of the negative impact of development programs in Africa that have emphasized rural areas and/or attempted to reintegrate youth into traditional social systems that are repressive and/or do not suit their needs.

35. See Singer, *Children at War.* One importance of Singer's work is that it begins to bridge the divide between security analysis and the child-soldiers literature.

36. See, for example, Wessells and Jonah, "Recruitment and Reintegration."

37. Berdal and Malone, eds., *Greed and Grievance.*

38. See World Bank, "Children and Youth."

39. Wolfensohn, "Remarks on Post-Conflict Peacebuilding."

40. La Cava, Clert, and Lytle, *Investing in Youth Empowerment and Inclusion.*

41. See, for example, Anderson, *Do No Harm.*

42. Bush and Saltarelli, *Two Faces of Education;* Tawil, Harley, and Porteous, *Curriculum Change and Social Cohesion;* Tawil and Harley, *Education, Conflict and Social Cohesion;* Smith and Vaux, *Education, Conflict and International Development;* L. Davis, *Conflict and Education;* Sommers, "Children, Education and War"; Buckland and Sommers, *Parallel Worlds;* Obura, *Never Again;* Sinclair, "Planning Education"; and World Bank, *Reshaping the Future.*

43. Sinclair, "Planning Education," 123.

44. L. Davis, *Conflict and Education.*

45. Sinclair, "Planning Education," 27.

46. Tibbitts, "Literature Review,'" 1–7.

47. Ibid.

48. Schell-Faucon, "Conflict Transformation."

49. Ibid.; E. Davis, "Strategies for Promoting Democracy in Iraq"; Adwan and Bar-On, "Sharing History."

50. Helsing, "Education, Sustainable Peace and Reconciliation."

51. McEvoy-Levy, ed., *Troublemakers or Peacemakers?*; Kemper, *Youth in War-to-Peace Transitions*; Weiss, *Perpetrating Power*; McIntyre and Thusi, "Children and Youth"; U.S. Agency for International Development, "Youth and Conflict." The last does not cite any post-conflict literature, though it seems to draw on internal agency knowledge and experience in post-conflict situations.

52. See McEvoy-Levy, ed., *Troublemakers or Peacemakers?*, and Kemper, *Youth in War-to-Peace Transitions*, on the latter question.

53. See Miall, Ramsbotham, and Woodhouse, *Contemporary Conflict Resolution*, and McEvoy-Levy, "Introduction."

54. McEvoy-Levy, ed., *Troublemakers or Peacemakers?*

55. A related approach can be found in Kemper, *Youth in War-to-Peace Transitions*, who examines the different approaches—rights-based, economic, and sociopolitical—of international organizations working with youth.

56. For further discussion of cultural and political influences of how "youth" is defined see McEvoy-Levy, ed., "Introduction."

57. Mawson, "Children, Impunity and Justice," 138.

58. Sekaggya, "Ugandan Children."

59. Sommers, "In the Shadow of Genocide," and Kruse, "Comoros." See also Mgbako, *"Ingando* Solidarity Camps."

60. Kruse, "Comoros."

61. United Nations Secretary General, *Children and Armed Conflict*, 30.

62. BBC News, "Ugandan Top Rebel Leader Indicted."

63. United Nations Secretary General, *Children and Armed Conflict*, and United Nations Office for the Coordination of Humanitarian Affairs, "Afghanistan."

64. United Nations Office for the Coordination of Humanitarian Affairs, "Afghanistan," 1.

65. W. Ross, "Congo's Battle with Disarmament," 1.

66. Wessells and Jonah, "Recruitment and Reintegration," 44–45.

67. McEvoy-Levy, "Politics, Protest and Local 'Power-Sharing.'"

68. See Cairns, *Children and Political Violence.*

69. Young prostitute in Freetown, Sierra Leone, quoted in Weiss, *Perpetrating Power*, 1.

70. Wessells and Jonah, "Recruitment and Reintegration."

71. Sanford, "Moral Imagination of Survival."

72. Sommers "Fearing Africa's Young Men," 2.

73. Kirlic in Helsing et al., "Young People's Activism," 201.

74. McEvoy-Levy, "Politics, Protest and Local 'Power-Sharing,'" and Cilliers, "Transforming Post-Accord Education Systems."

75. Sommers, *Urbanization, War, and Africa's Youth at Risk*, and McEvoy-Levy, "Silenced Voices."

76. McEvoy-Levy, "Silenced Voices."

77. Wessells and Jonah, "Recruitment and Reintegration."

78. Straker et al., *Faces in the Revolution;* Cairns, *Children and Political Violence;* Barber, "Political Violence, Family Relations, and Palestinian Youth Functioning"; Ziv, Kruglanski, and Schulman, "Children's Psychological Reactions to Wartime Stress."

79. See Adwan and Bar-On, "Sharing History"; Senehi and Byrne, "From Violence Toward Peace"; Cilliers, "Transforming Post-Accord Education Systems"; and McEvoy-Levy, "Politics, Protest and Local 'Power-Sharing.'"

80. The cases of young anti-apartheid activists in South Africa and youth involved in first intifada provide good examples of this and are discussed in McEvoy-Levy, "Introduction."

81. McEvoy-Levy, ed., "Troublemakers or Peacemakers, 151–52, 1, 56.

82. United Nations Department of Economic and Social Affairs, *World Youth Report 2005,* Section 32.

83. S/RES/1379 2001. 8(e), p. 3. Available at the Web site of the United Nations Office for the Coordination of Humanitarian Affairs, http://ochaonline.un.org/webpage.asp?Page=1790.

84. The Sierra Leone case has been mentioned as an example where significant implementation of youth participation initiatives has taken place: "Most youth in places such as Makeni were of the opinion that before the war they were hardly involved (if at all) in decision making in their communities. The positive outcome of the war was that it made people in positions of authority in government and the community realise that without involving the youth in social and political life there is no way peace could be sustained." McIntrye and Thusi, "Children and Youth," 78. See also Hope-Sierra Leone, "Report of the Youth Peace Symposium."

85. McIntrye and Thusi, "Children and Youth," 77.

86. McIntrye and Thusi, "Children and Youth."

87. Straker et al., *Faces in the Revolution;* Cairns, *Children and Political Violence;* Barber, "Political Violence, Family Relations, and Palestinian Youth Functioning."

88. McEvoy-Levy, "Conclusion."

89. Wessells and Jonah, "Recruitment and Reintegration."

90. Sonnenschein in Helsing et al., "Young People's Activism."

91. Kirlic in Helsing et al., "Young People's Activism."

92. Kirlic and McMaster in Helsing et al., "Young People's Activism."

93. Sonnenschein in Helsing et al., "Young People's Activism"; and Sanford, "Moral Imagination of Survival."

94. Nordstrom, "Jagged Edge of Peace."

95. Eoin O'Broin, interview with Siobhán McEvoy-Levy, June 2001.

96. Adwan and Bar-On, "Sharing History."

97. Ibid.

98. See also McEvoy-Levy, "Silenced Voices."

99. It is not assumed that this is the only or best possible model for reconstruction. The goal here is to apply a youth-centered analysis to an influential reconstruction approach and make an initial exploration of the outcomes.

100. Quoted in Weiss, *Perpetrating Power,* 9.

AFTERWORD

1. Hampson, *Nurturing Peace.*

2. Crocker and Hampson with Aall, eds., *Managing Global Chaos.*

3. Walter, "Critical Barrier"; Stedman, "Introduction."

4. Iraq is slightly different, however, in that no agreement preceded the peacebuilding efforts; such an agreement has been cobbled together during the peacebuilding process but is still very unstable as of this writing.

5. The literature on separate elements of peacebuilding is quite extensive. Some examples include: Ball and Helavy, *Making Peace Work;* Hayner, "Fifteen Truth Commissions"; Oakley, Goldberg, and Dziedzic, eds., *Policing the New World Disorder.*

6. One excellent example is a critical analysis of human rights advocacy in the post-settlement period. See Putnam, "Human Rights and Sustainable Peace."

7. Hodgkins, Allison, "Guns for Promises: How Peace Agreements Institutionalize Power Asymmetry in Armed Self-Determination Conflicts," dissertation proposal submitted to the Fletcher School of Law and Diplomacy, Medford, MA, 2006. (Document on file with author.)

8. Some of the organizations that have devoted significant resources to evaluation are the UN Development Program (UNDP), the Organization for Economic Cooperation and Development (OECD), the U.S. Agency for International Development (AID), and Britain's Department for International Development (DFID).

9. Church and Rogers, *Designing for Results.* See also Anderson, "Experiences with Impact Assessment."

10. Aucoin and Babbitt, *Transitional Justice.*

11. Independent Evaluation of the National Youth Policy in Bosnia-Herzegovina (2005), prepared by the Youth Information Agency, Sarajevo, Bosnia-Herzegovina. Accessed on July 28, 2006 at:
http://www.un.org/esa/socdev/unyin/documents/wpaysubmissions/bosnia.pdf.

12. Aucoin and Babbitt, *Transitional Justice.*

13. C. Bell, *Peace Agreements,* 304.

14. United Nations Security Council. Resolution 1325.

Bibliography

Adwan, Sami, and Dan Bar-On. "Sharing History: Palestinian and Israeli Teachers and Pupils Learning Each Other's Narrative." In *Troublemakers or Peacemakers? Youth and Post-Accord Peace Building*, edited by Siobhán McEvoy-Levy, 217–34. Notre Dame, IN: University of Notre Dame Press, 2006.

Anderson, Mary B. *Do No Harm*. Boulder, CO: Lynne Rienner, 1999.

———. "Experiences with Impact Assessment: Can We Know What Good We Do?" Berghof Research Center for Constructive Conflict Management. Available at: http://www.berghof-handbook.net.

Apfel, Roberta J., and Bennett Simon. *Minefields in the Hearts: The Mental Health of Children in War and Communal Violence*. New Haven: Yale University Press, 1996.

Arafat, Cairo, with Neil Boothby. "A Psychosocial Assessment of Palestinian Children." U.S. Agency for International Development report, July 2003. http://www.usaid.gov/wbg/reports/Final_CPSP_Assessment_English.pdf.

Arnson, Cynthia J., and I. William Zartman. *Rethinking the Economics of War: The Intersection of Need, Creed and Greed*. Washington, DC: Woodrow Wilson Center Press, 2005.

Aspen Institute. *State Crimes: Punishment or Pardon. Papers and Reports of the Conference, November 4–6, 1988*. Queenstown, MD: The Justice and Society Program of the Aspen Institute, 1989.

Aucoin, Louis, and Eileen Babbitt. *Transitional Justice: Assessment Survey of Conditions in the Former Yugoslavia*. Belgrade: UN Development Program, 2006.

Ball, Nicole, and Tammy Helavy. *Making Peace Work: The Role of the International Development Community*. Policy Essay No. 18. Washington, DC: Overseas Development Council, 1996.

Barber, Brian K. "Political Violence, Family Relations, and Palestinian Youth Functioning." *Journal of Adolescent Research* 14 (April 1999): 206–31.

Bartkus, Viva Ona. *The Dynamic of Secession*. Cambridge, England: Cambridge University Press, 1999.

Baxter, Victoria. "Empirical Research Methodologies of Transitional Justice Mechanisms: Conference Report." Conference sponsored by the Science and Human Rights Program of the American Association for the Advancement of Sciences (AAAS) and the Centre for the Study of Violence and Reconciliation (CSVR), Stellenbosch, South Africa, November 2002. http://shr.aaas.org/transitionaljustice/mtjm.

BBC News. "Ugandan Top Rebel Leader Indicted." October 7, 2005. http://news.bbc.co.uk/1/hi/world/africa/4320124.stm (accessed May 7, 2006).

Bell, Christine. *Peace Agreements and Human Rights.* Oxford: Oxford University Press, 2000.

Bell, Desmond. *Acts of Union: Youth Culture and Sectarianism in Northern Ireland.* London: Macmillan, 1990.

Bender, L., and J. Frosch. "Children's Reactions to the War." *American Journal of Orthopsychiatry* 22 (1942): 571–86.

Berdal, Mats, and David M. Malone, eds. *Greed and Grievance: Economic Agendas in Civil Wars.* Boulder, CO: Lynne Rienner, 2000.

Boothby, Neil, and C. Knudsen. "Children of the Gun." *Scientific American* 282 (January 2000): 40–45.

Boraine, Alex. "Transitional Justice as an Emerging Field." Paper presented at the conference "Repairing the Past: Reparations and Transitions to Democracy," Ottawa, Canada, March 2004. http://www.gender-budgets.org/uploads/user-S/10829975041revised-boraine-ottawa-2004.pdf.

Borchini, Charles, Stephanie Lanz, and Erin O'Connell. "Child Soldiers: Implications for U.S. Forces." Cultural Intelligence Seminar Series Report CETO 005-02. Quantico, VA: Center for Emerging Threats and Opportunities, November 2002.

Borer, Tristan Anne. "Truth Commissions." In *The Essential Guide to Human Rights*, edited by Christien van den Anker and Rhona Smith, 338–340. London: Hodder Arnold, 2005.

———. "Truth Telling as a Peace-Building Activity: A Theoretical Overview." In *Telling the Truths: Truth Telling and Peace Building in Post-Conflict Societies*, edited by Tristan Anne Borer, 1–57. Notre Dame, IN: University of Notre Dame Press, 2006.

———, ed. *Telling the Truths: Truth Telling and Peace Building in Post-Conflict Societies.* Notre Dame, IN: University of Notre Dame Press, 2006.

Boyden, Jo, and Joanna de Berry, eds. *Children and Youth on the Front Line: Ethnography, Armed Conflict, and Displacement.* New York: Berghahn Books, 2004.

Bracken, Patrick. "The Rehabilitation of Child Soldiers: Defining Needs and Appropriate Responses." *Medicine, Conflict and Survival* 12 (April/June 1996): 1362–69.

Brahm, Eric. "Getting to the Bottom of Truth: Examining Truth Commission Success and Impact." Paper presented at the International Studies Association Annual Meeting, Honolulu, February 2005.

Braungart, Margaret, and Richard Braungart. "Black and White South African University Students' Perceptions of Self and Country: An Exploratory Study." *South African Journal of Sociology* 24 (1995): 134–48.

Brett, Rachel, and Margaret McCallin. *Children: The Invisible Soldiers.* Vaxjo, Sweden: Rädda Barnen, 1998.

Brett, Rachel, and Irma Sprecht. *Young Soldiers: Why They Choose to Fight.* Boulder, CO: Lynne Rienner, 2004.

Buckland, Peter, and Marc Sommers. *Parallel Worlds: Rebuilding the Education System in Kosovo.* Paris: UNESCO International Institute for Educational Planning, 2004.

Bush, Kenneth D., and Diana Saltarelli, eds. *The Two Faces of Education in Ethnic Conflict: Towards a Peacebuilding Education for Children.* Florence, Italy: UNICEF Innocenti Research Centre, 2000.

Byrne, Sean. *Growing Up in a Divided Society: The Influence of Conflict on Belfast Schoolchildren.* Cranbury, NJ: Associated University Presses, 1997.

Cairns, Ed. *Caught in the Crossfire: Children and the Northern Ireland Conflict.* Belfast, Northern Ireland, and Syracuse, NY: Appletree and Syracuse University Press, 1987.

———. *Children and Political Violence.* Oxford, England: Blackwell, 1996.

Cairns, Ed, Frances McLernon, Wendy Moore, and Ilse Hakvoort. "The Impact of the Peace Process in Northern Ireland on Children's and Adolescents' Ideas about War and Peace." In *Troublemakers or Peacemakers? Youth and Post-Accord Peace Building,* edited by Siobhán McEvoy-Levy, 117–38. Notre Dame, IN: University of Notre Dame Press, 2006.

Call, Charles T., and William Stanley. "Military and Police Reform after Civil Wars." In *Contemporary Peacemaking: Conflict, Violence, and Peace Processes,* edited by John Darby and Roger Mac Ginty, 212–23. London and New York: Palgrave Macmillan, 2003.

Cameron, Sara. "The Role of Children as Peace-Makers in Colombia." *Development* 43 (2000): 40–45.

Carpenter, R. Charli, ed. *Born of War: Sexual Violence, Children's Human Rights and the Global Community.* Bloomfield, CT: Kumarian Press, forthcoming.

Church, Cheyanne, and Mark Rogers. *Designing for Results: Integrating Monitoring and Evaluation in Conflict Transformation Programs.* Washington, DC: Search for Common Ground, 2006. Available at: http://www.sfcg.org/programmes/ilr/ilt_manualpage.html.

Cilliers, Jaco. "Transforming Post-Accord Education Systems: Local Reflections from Bosnia-Herzegovina." In *Troublemakers or Peacemakers? Youth and Post-Accord Peace Building,* edited by Siobhán McEvoy-Levy, 173–94. Notre Dame, IN: University of Notre Dame Press, 2006.

Cincotta, Richard. "Youth Bulge, Underemployment Raise Risks of Civil Conflict." Worldwatch State of the World Global Security Brief # 2, March 2005. http://www.worldwatch.org/features/security/briefs/2/ (accessed April 2006).

Cincotta, Richard P., Robert Engelman, and Daniele Anastasion. *The Security Demographic: Population and Civil Conflict after the Cold War.* Washington, DC: Population Action International, 2003.

Cohn, Ilene, and Guy Goodwin-Gill. *Child Soldiers: The Role of Children in Armed Conflicts.* New York: Oxford Clarendon Press/Henry Dunant Institute, 1994.

Collier, Paul, and Anke Hoeffler. "Greed and Grievance in Civil War." World Bank Working Paper, October 21, 2001. http://www.worldbank.org/research/conflict/papers/greedgrievance_23oct.pdf.

Connolly, Paul, and Paul McGinn. *Sectarianism, Children and Community Relations in Northern Ireland.* Coleraine, Northern Ireland: Centre for the Study of Conflict/University of Ulster, 1999.

Cox, Michael, Adrian Guelke, and Fiona Stephen, eds. *A Farewell to Arms? Beyond the Good Friday Agreement.* Manchester, England: Manchester University Press, 2000.

Crane, David. "Dancing with the Devil: Prosecuting West Africa's Warlords, Current Lessons Learned and Challenges." Paper presented at the Colloquium of Prosecutors of International Criminal Tribunals, Arusha, Tanzania, November 25–27, 2004. Available at http://69.94.11.53/ENGLISH/colloquium04/Crane.htm.

Crocker, Chester A. and Fen Osler Hampson, with Pamela R. Aall, eds. *Managing Global Chaos: Sources of and Responses to International Conflict*. Washington, DC: U.S. Institute of Peace Press, 1996.

Darby, John. *The Effects of Violence on Peace Processes*. Washington, DC: U.S. Institute of Peace Press, 2001.

———, ed. *Violence and Reconstruction*. Notre Dame, IN: University of Notre Dame Press, 2006.

Darby, John, and Roger Mac Ginty, eds. *The Management of Peace Processes*. London and New York: Palgrave Macmillan, 2000.

———, eds. *Contemporary Peacemaking: Conflict, Violence and Peace Processes*. London and New York: Palgrave Macmillan, 2003.

Davis, Eric. "Strategies for Promoting Democracy in Iraq." USIP Special Report No. 153, October 2005. http://www.usip.org/pubs/specialreports/sr153.html.

Davis, Lynn. *Conflict and Education: Complexity and Chaos*. London: Routledge, 2004.

Dawes, Alan, and D. Donald, eds. *Children and Adversity: Psychological Perspectives on South African Research*. Cape Town, South Africa: David Philip, 1994.

Dennis, Michael. "Newly Adopted Protocols to the Convention on the Rights of the Child." *American Journal of International Law* 94 (October 2000): 789–96.

Dissel, Amanda. "Youth, Street Gangs and Violence in South Africa." In *Youth, Street Culture and Urban Violence in Africa*. Proceedings of the international symposium held in Abidjan, Côte d'Ivoire, May 5–7, 1997. Johannesburg, South Africa: Centre for the Study of Violence and Reconciliation, 1997.

Dougherty, Beth K. "Pursuing Justice on a Shoestring: The Case of Sierra Leone." Paper presented at the International Studies Association Annual Meeting, Honolulu, February 2005.

Doyle, Michael, Ian Johnstone, and Robert Orr, eds. *Keeping the Peace: Multidimensional UN Operations in Cambodia and El Salvador*. Cambridge, England: Cambridge University Press, 1997.

Du Toit, Pierre. "South Africa: In Search of Post-Settlement Peace." In *The Management of Peace Processes*, edited by John Darby and Roger Mac Ginty, 16–60. London and New York: Palgrave Macmillan, 2000.

———. *South Africa's Brittle Peace: The Problem of Post-Settlement Violence*. London: Palgrave, 2001.

——. "Why Post-Settlement Settlements?" *Journal of Democracy* 14 (2003): 104–18.

The Economist, "Uneasy Peace in Guatemala," June 28, 1997.

Eyber, Carola, and Alastair Ager. "Researching Young People's Experiences of War: Participatory Methods and the Trauma Discourse in Angola." In *Children and Youth on the Frontline: Ethnography, Armed Conflict, and Displacement*, edited by Jo Boyden and Joanna de Berry, 189–208. New York: Berghahn Books, 2004.

Freeman, Mark. "The Essentials of Transitional Justice." Workshop sponsored by the International Center for Transitional Justice, Leuven, Belgium, February 2–5, 2006.

Gamba, Virginia. "Post-Agreement Demobilization, Disarmament, and Reconstruction: Towards a New Approach." In *Violence and Reconstruction*, edited by John Darby, 53–76. Notre Dame, IN: University of Notre Dame Press, 2006.

Garbarino, James, and Kathleen Kostelny. "What Children Can Tell Us about Living in a War Zone." In *Children in a Violent Society*, edited by J. D. Osofsky, 32–41. New York: Guilford Press, 1997.

Garton Ash, Timothy. "True Confessions." *New York Review of Books* 44, no. 12 (July 17, 1997): 36.

Geller, Daniel S., and J. David Singer. *Nations at War: A Scientific Study of International Conflict*. Cambridge, England: Cambridge University Press, 1998.

Gillespie, James M., and Gordon M. Allport. *Youth's Outlook on the Future: A Cross-National Study*. New York: Doubleday, 1950.

Goldblatt, Beth and Sheila Meintjes. "South African Women Demand the Truth." In *What Women Do in Wartime: Gender and Conflict in Africa*, edited by Meredeth Turshen and Clotilde Twagiramariya, 27–61. New York: Zed Books, 1998.

Gurr, Ted Robert. *Minorities at Risk: A Global View of Ethnopolitical Conflicts*. Washington, DC: U.S. Institute of Peace Press, 1993.

Haass, Richard N. *Conflicts Unending: The United States and Regional Disputes*. New Haven, CT: Yale University Press, 1990.

Hakvoort, Ilse. "Children's Conceptions of Peace and War: A Longitudinal Study." *Peace and Conflict: Journal of Peace Psychology* 2 (1995): 1–15.

Hakvoort, Ilse, and Louis Oppenheimer. "Children and Adolescents' Conceptions of Peace, War, and Strategies to Attain Peace: A Dutch Case Study." *Journal of Peace Research* 30 (1993): 65–77.

Hall, Robin. "How Children Think and Feel about War and Peace: An Australian Study." *Journal of Peace Research* 30 (1993): 181–96.

Hampson, Fen Osler. *Nurturing Peace: Why Peace Settlements Succeed or Fail.* Washington, DC: U.S. Institute of Peace Press, 1996.

Harbinson, Jeremy, and Joan Harbinson, eds. *A Society under Stress: Children and Young People in Northern Ireland*, Somerset, England: Open Books, 1980.

Harbom, Lotta, and Peter Wallensteen. "Armed Conflict and Its International Dimensions, 1946–2004." *Journal of Peace Research* 42 (2005): 623–35.

Hart, Jason. "Beyond Struggle and Aid: Children's Identities in a Palestinian Refugee Camp." In *Children and Youth on the Front Line: Ethnography, Armed Conflict, and Displacement*, edited by Jo Boyden and Joanna de Berry, 167–88. New York: Berghahn Books, 2004.

Hartzell, Caroline, Mathew Hoddie, and Donald Rothchild. "Stabilizing the Peace after Civil War: An Investigation of Some Key Variables." *International Organization* 55 (Winter 2001): 183–208.

Hayner, Priscilla B. "Fifteen Truth Commissions, 1974–1994: A Comparative Study." *Human Rights Quarterly* 16, no. 4. (1994): 597–655.

———. "International Guidelines for the Creation and Operation of Truth Commissions: A Preliminary Proposal." *Law and Contemporary Problems* 59 (Autumn 1996): 173–80.

———. *Unspeakable Truths: Confronting State Terror and Atrocity.* New York: Routledge, 2001.

Helsing, Jeffrey. "Education, Sustainable Peace and Reconciliation." Paper presented at the annual meeting of the International Studies Association, San Diego, CA, March 22, 2006.

Helsing, Jeffrey, Namik Kirlic, Neil McMaster, and Nir Sonnenschein. 2006. "Young People's Activism and the Transition to Peace: Bosnia, Northern Ireland and Israel." In *Troublemakers or Peacemakers? Youth and Post-Accord Peace Building*, edited by Siobhán McEvoy-Levy, 195–216. Notre Dame, IN: University of Notre Dame Press, 2006.

Heppner, Kevin. *"My Gun Was as Tall as Me": Child Soldiers in Burma.* New York: Human Rights Watch, 2002.

Hermann, Tamar, and David Newman. "A Path Strewn with Thorns: Along the Difficult Road of Israeli-Palestinian Peacemaking." In *The Management of Peace Processes*, edited by John Darby and Roger Mac Ginty, 107–53. New York and London: Palgrave Macmillan, 2000.

Höglund, Kristine, and I. William Zartman. "Violence by the State: Official Spoilers and Their Allies." In *Violence and Reconstruction*, edited by John Darby, 11–32. Notre Dame, IN: University of Notre Dame Press, 2006.

Høiskar, Astri Halsan. "Underage and Under Fire: An Enquiry into the Use of Child Soldiers, 1994–98." *Childhood* 8 (August 2001): 340–62.

Hope–Sierra Leone. "Report of the Youth Peace Symposium in Makeni, Sierra Leone," May 18, 2001. http://www.hopesierraleone.org/youth_sympos_.html (accessed May 6, 2006).

Human Rights Watch. *The Human Rights Watch Global Report on Women's Human Rights.* New York: Human Rights Watch, 1995.

Huyse, Luc. "Dealing with the Past and Imaging the Future." In *Peacebuilding: A Field Guide*, edited by Luc Reychler and Thania Paffenholz, 322–29. Boulder, CO: Lynne Rienner, 2002.

Inter-American Court on Human Rights. Velásquez Rodríguez case, Judgment of July 29, 1988, Ser. C, no. 4 (1988). http://www1.umn.edu/humanrts/iachr/b_11_12d.htm.

International Center for Transitional Justice. *Annual Report.* New York: ICTJ, 2004.

Jagodic, G. K. "Is War a Good or a Bad Thing? The Attitudes of Croatian, Israeli, and Palestinian Children towards War." *International Journal of Psychology* 35 (2000): 241–57.

Jarman, Neil. *Managing Disorder: Responding to Interface Violence in North Belfast.* Belfast, Northern Ireland: Office of the First Minister and Deputy First Minister, 2002.

Jeong, Ho-Won. *Peacebuilding in Postconflict Societies.* Boulder, CO: Lynne Rienner, 2005.

Jones, Lynne. "Adolescent Understandings of Political Violence and Their Relationship to Mental Health: A Qualitative Study of Bosnia Herzegovina." Paper submitted to the International Conference on War-Affected Children, Winnipeg, Canada, September 11–17, 2000. http://www.waraffectedchildren.gc.ca/socscimedpaper-en.asp (accessed May 6, 2006).

Kalshoven, Frits. "Child Soldiers: The Role of Children in Armed Conflicts." *American Journal of International Law* 89 (October 1995): 849–52.

Keairns, Yvonne. *The Voices of Girl Child Soldiers: Colombia.* New York: Quaker United Nations Office, January 2003.

Kemper, Yvonne. *Youth in War-to-Peace Transitions: Approaches of International Organizations.* Berghof Report No. 10. Berlin: Berghof Research Center for Constructive Conflict Management, 2005. http://www.berghof-center.org/publications/reports/complete/BR10e.pdf (accessed May 2, 2006).

Klare, Michael. "The Kalashnikov Age." *Bulletin of Atomic Scientists* 55 (1999): 18–22.

Kriesberg, Louis. *Constructive Conflicts: From Escalation to Resolution,* 2nd ed. New York: Rowman and Littlefield, 2003.

Kroc Institute for International Peace Studies. "The Horizon of Peacebuilding: The Strategic Challenges of Post-Agreement Change." *Peace Colloquy* 3 (Summer 2003): 17.

Kruse, Aurelien. "Comoros: What to Do with Ex-Militia Youth?" PCF Occasional Note No 4. Washington, DC: World Bank, January 2004.

Kurtenbach, Sabine. "Dealing with the Past in Latin America." In *Peacebuilding: A Field Guide,* edited by Luc Reychler and Thania Paffenholz, 352–57. Boulder, CO: Lynne Rienner, 2002.

La Cava, Gloria, Corine Clert, and Paula Lytle. *Investing in Youth Empowerment and Inclusion: A Social Development Approach.* Social Development Paper No. 60. Washington, DC: World Bank, February 2004.

Leebaw, Bronwyn Anne. "New Approaches to Transitional Justice: Combining Restorative Justice and Prosecution." Paper presented at the International Studies Association Annual Meeting, Montreal, 2004.

Licklider, Roy. "The Consequences of Negotiated Settlements in Civil Wars, 1945–1993." *American Political Science Review* 89 (September 1995), 681–90.

Mac Ginty, Roger. "Biting the Bullet: Decommissioning in the Transition from War to Peace in Northern Ireland." *Irish Studies in International Affairs* (1999): 237–47.

———. *No War, No Peace: The Rejuvenation of Peace Processes and Peace Accords.* London: Palgrave, 2006.

———. "Post-Accord Crime." In *Violence and Reconstruction,* edited by John Darby, 101–20. Notre Dame, IN: University of Notre Dame Press, 2006.

Machel, Graça. *Impact of Armed Conflict on Children.* Document A/51/306. New York: United Nations, 1996. http://www.unicef.org/graca/

Maoz, Ifat. "Multiple Conflicts and Competing Agendas: A Framework for Conceptualizing Structured Encounters between Groups in Conflict—The Case of a Coexistence Project between Jews and Palestinians in Israel." *Journal of Peace Psychology* 6 (2000): 135–56.

Marks, Monique. *Young Warriors: Youth Politics, Identity and Violence in South Africa.* Johannesburg, South Africa: Witwatersrand University Press, 2001.

Maslen, S., and S. Islamshah. "Revolution Not Evolution: Protecting the Rights of Children in Armed Conflicts in the New Millennium." *Development* 43 (March 2000): 28–31.

Mawson, Andrew. "Children, Impunity and Justice: Some Dilemmas from Northern Uganda." In *Children and Youth on the Front Line: Ethnography, Armed Conflict, and Displacement,* edited by Jo Boyden and Joanna de Berry, 130–41. New York: Berghahn Books, 2004.

McEvoy-Levy, Siobhán. "Communities and Peace: Young Catholics in Northern Ireland." *Journal of Peace Research* 37 (2000): 85–104.

———. "Conclusion: Youth and Post-Accord Peace Building." In *Troublemakers or Peacemakers? Youth and Post-Accord Peace Building,* edited by Siobhán McEvoy-Levy, 139–72. Notre Dame, IN: University of Notre Dame Press, 2006.

———. "Introduction: Youth and the Post-Accord Environment." In *Troublemakers or Peacemakers? Youth and Post-Accord Peace Building,* edited by Siobhán McEvoy-Levy, 1–26. Notre Dame, IN: University of Notre Dame Press, 2006.

———. "Politics, Protest and Local 'Power-Sharing' in North Belfast." In *Troublemakers or Peacemakers? Youth and Post-Accord Peace Building,* edited by Siobhán McEvoy-Levy, 139–71. Notre Dame, IN: University of Notre Dame Press, 2006.

———. "Silenced Voices? Youth and Peer Relationships in Armed Conflict and its Aftermath." In *A World Turned Upside Down: Social Ecological Approaches to Children in War Zones,* edited by Neil Boothby, Alison Strang, and Michael Wessells. Bloomfield, CT: Kumarian 2006.

———. "Youth, Violence and Conflict Transformation." *Peace Review: A Transnational Quarterly* 13 (March 2001): 89–96.

———, ed. *Troublemakers or Peacemakers? Youth and Post-Accord Peace Building.* Notre Dame, IN: University of Notre Dame Press, 2006.

McIntyre, Angela. "Rights, Roots Causes and Recruitment: The Youth Factor in Africa's Armed Conflicts." *African Security Review* 12 (2003): 91–99. http://www.iss.co.za/pubs/ASR/12No2/E4.pdf.

McIntyre, Angela, and Thokozani Thusi. "Children and Youth in Sierra Leone's Peacebuilding Process." *African Security Review* 12 (2003): 73–80. http://www.iss.co.za/pubs/ASR/12No2/E2.pdf.

McLernon, F., N. Ferguson, and E. Cairns. "Comparison of Northern Irish Children's Attitudes to War and Peace before and after the Paramilitary Ceasefires." *International Journal of Behavioral Development* 20 (1997): 715–30.

Mendeloff, David. "Truth-Seeking, Truth-Telling, and Postconflict Peacebuilding: Curb the Enthusiasm?" *International Studies Review* 6 (2004): 355–80.

Méndez, Juan E. "The Human Right to Truth: Lessons Learned from Latin American Experiences with Truth Telling." In *Telling the Truths: Truth Telling and Peace Building in Post-Conflict Societies,* edited by Tristan Anne Borer, 115–50. Notre Dame, IN: University of Notre Dame Press, 2006.

Mgbako, Chi. "Ingando Solidarity Camps: Reconciliation and Political Indoctrination in Post-Genocide Rwanda." *Harvard Human Rights Journal* 18 (2005): 201–24.

Miall, Hugh, Oliver Ramsbotham, and Tom Woodhouse. *Contemporary Conflict Resolution: The Prevention, Management and Transformation of Deadly Conflicts.* Cambridge, UK: Polity Press, 1999.

Morkel, S. "Peace Dividends: The South African Experience." In *Coming Out of Violence: Peace Dividends,* edited by John Darby, 12–21. Derry, Northern Ireland: INCORE, 1995.

Murray, Dominic. "Post-Accord Police Reform." In *Violence and Reconstruction,* edited by John Darby, 77–100. Notre Dame, IN: University of Notre Dame Press, 2006.

Nordstrom, Carolyn. "The Jagged Edge of Peace: The Creation of Culture and War Orphans in Angola." In *Troublemakers or Peacemakers? Youth and Post-Accord Peace Building,* edited by Siobhán McEvoy-Levy, 99–116. Notre Dame, IN: University of Notre Dame Press, 2006.

Northern Ireland Statistics and Research Agency. *Annual Abstract of Statistics,* vol. 16. Belfast: NISRA, 1998.

Oakley, Robert B., Eliot M. Goldberg, and Michael J. Dziedzic, eds. *Policing the New World Disorder: Peace Operations and Public Security.* Washington, DC: National Defense University Press, 1998.

Obura, Anna. *Never Again: Educational Reconstruction in Rwanda.* Paris: International Institute for Educational Planning (UNESCO), 2003.

Perriello, Tom, and Marieke Wierda. *The Special Court for Sierra Leone under Scrutiny*. Prosecutions Case Studies Series. New York: International Center for Transitional Justice, 2006.
http://www.ictj.org/static/Prosecutions/Sierra.study.pdf.

Peters, Joel. *Pathways to Peace: The Multilateral Arab-Israeli Peace Talks*. London: Royal Institute of International Affairs, 1996.

PIOOM (The International Research Program on Root Causes of Human Rights Violations) Databank. *PIOOM World Conflict Map*. Leiden, The Netherlands: University of Leiden Press, 2000.

Police Service of Northern Ireland. *Crime Statistics for Northern Ireland* (updated annually).
http://www.psni.police.uk/index/statistics_branch/pg_crime_stats.htm.

Punamaki, Raija-Leena. *Childhood under Conflict: The Attitudes and Emotional Life of Israeli and Palestinian Children*. University of Tampere, Finland: Tampere Peace Research Institute, 1987.

Putnam, Tonya L. "Human Rights and Sustainable Peace." In *Ending Civil Wars: The Implementation of Peace Agreements*, edited by Stephen J. Stedman, Donald Rothchild, and Elizabeth M. Cousens, 237–71. Boulder, CO: Lynne Rienner, 2002.

Raviv, Amiram, Louis Oppenheimer, and Daniel Bar-Tal, eds. *How Children Understand War and Peace: A Call for International Peace Education*. San Francisco: Jossey-Bass Publishers, 1999.

Reed, John. "Mbeki Confident as Serious Crime Falls." *Financial Times*, February 12, 2005.

Richards, Paul. *Fighting for the Rain Forest: War, Youth and Resources in Sierra Leone*. Oxford: James Currey, 1996.

Richmond, Oliver P. *The Transformation of Peace*. London and New York: Palgrave Macmillan, 2005.

Rigby, Andrew. *Justice and Reconciliation: After the Violence*. Boulder, CO: Lynne Rienner, 2001.

Rohter, Larry. "Like Carrot, Stick Fails with Rebels in Colombia." *New York Times*, September 25, 1999, A9.

Ross, Fiona C. *Bearing Witness: Women and the Truth and Reconciliation Commission in South Africa*. Sterling, VA: Pluto Press, 2003.

Ross, Will. "Congo's Battle with Disarmament." BBC News online, June 9, 2005.
http://news.bbc.co.uk/1/hi/world/africa/4073862.stm (accessed May 7, 2006).

Rotberg, Robert I., and Dennis Thompson, eds. *Truth v. Justice: The Morality of Truth Commissions.* Princeton: Princeton University Press, 2000.

Sanford, Victoria. *Buried Secrets: Truth and Human Rights in Guatemala.* London: Palgrave Macmillan, 2003.

———. "The Moral Imagination of Survival: Displacement and Child Soldiers in Guatemala and Colombia." In *Troublemakers or Peacemakers? Youth and Post-Accord Peace Building*, edited by Siobhán McEvoy-Levy, 49–80. Notre Dame, IN: University of Notre Dame Press, 2006.

Schell-Faucon, Stephanie. "Conflict Transformation through Education and Youth Programmes." Berlin, Germany: Berghof Research Center for Constructive Conflict Management, 2001. http://www.berghof-handbook.net/articles/schell_faucon_hb.pdf.

Sekaggya, Liza. "Ugandan Children Born in Captivity and Their Human Rights." Comment during presentation at "'War Babies': Human Rights of Children Born of Wartime Rape and Sexual Exploitation" Interdisciplinary Workshop, University of Pittsburgh, November 13, 2004.

Senehi, Jessica, and Sean Byrne. "From Violence Toward Peace: The Role of Storytelling for Youth Healing and Political Empowerment after Social Conflict." In *Troublemakers or Peacemakers? Youth and Post-Accord Peace Building*, edited by Siobhán McEvoy-Levy, 235–58. Notre Dame, IN: University of Notre Dame Press, 2006.

Shaw, Rosalind. "Rethinking Truth and Reconciliation Commissions: Lessons from Sierra Leone." United States Institute of Peace Special Report No. 130. Washington, DC: USIP, February 2005. http://www.usip.org/pubs/specialreports/sr130.pdf.

Sierra Leone Truth and Reconciliation Commission Act. 2000. http://www.usip.org/library/tc/doc/charters/tc_sierra_leone_02102000.html.

Sinclair, Margaret. "Planning Education in and after Emergencies." Fundamentals of Education Planning Series, no. 73. Paris: International Institute for Education Planning (UNESCO), 2002. http://unesdoc.unesco.org/images/0012/001293/129356e.pdf.

Singer, Peter W. *Children at War.* New York: Pantheon, 2005.

Sisk, Timothy. *Democratization in South Africa: The Elusive Social Contract.* Princeton: Princeton University Press, 1995.

———. "Political Violence after Peace Talks: Searching for the Silver Lining." In *Violence and Reconstruction*, edited by John Darby, 121–42. Notre Dame, IN: University of Notre Dame Press, 2006.

Smith, Alan, and Tony Vaux. *Education, Conflict and International Development.* London: Department for International Development, February 2003.

Smyth, Marie. *Half the Battle: Understanding the Effects of the 'Troubles' on Children and Young People in Northern Ireland.* Derry: INCORE, 1998.

Smyth, Marie, with Marie Therese Fay, Emily Brough, and Jennifer Hamilton. *The Impact of Political Conflict on Children in Northern Ireland: A Report on the Community Conflict Impact on Children Study.* Belfast, Northern Ireland: Institute for Conflict Research, March 2004.

Somasundaram, Daya. "Child Soldiers: Understanding the Context." *British Medical Journal* 324 (May 2002): 1268–72.

Sommers, Marc. "Children, Education and War: Reaching Education For All (EFA) Objectives in Countries Affected by Conflict." Working Paper No. 1. Washington, DC: World Bank Conflict Prevention and Reconstruction Unit, 2002.

———. *Fear in Bongoland: Burundi Refugees in Urban Tanzania.* New York and Oxford: Berghahn Books, 2001.

———. "Fearing Africa's Young Men: The Case of Rwanda." Working Paper No. 32. Washington, DC: World Bank Conflict Prevention and Reconstruction Unit, 2006.

———. "In the Shadow of Genocide: Rwanda's Youth Challenge." In *Troublemakers or Peacemakers? Youth and Post-Accord Peace Building,* edited by Siobhán McEvoy-Levy, 81–98. Notre Dame, IN: University of Notre Dame Press, 2006.

———. *Urbanization, War, and Africa's Youth at Risk: Towards Understanding and Addressing Future Challenges.* Washington, DC: Basic Education and Support Policy, U.S. Agency for International Support, 2003.

Sooka, Yasmin. "Building Peace through Accountability—A Comparative Experience Between South Africa and Sierra Leone." Paper presented at "Peace Needs Women and Women Need Justice: A Conference on Gender Justice in Post-Conflict Situations," New York, September 2004. http://www.womenwarpeace.org/issues/justice/gjc_indextospeakers.htm.

South African Police Service. *Crime Statistics,* 2004. http://www.saps.gov.za/statistics/reports/crimestats/2004/crime_stats.htm.

Spielmann, Miriam. "If Peace Comes . . . : Future Expectations of Israeli Children and Youth." *Journal of Peace Research* 23 (1986): 51–67.

Stedman, Stephen J. "Introduction." In *Ending Civil Wars: The Implementation of Peace Agreements*, edited by Stephen J. Stedman, Donald Rothchild, and Elizabeth M. Cousens, 1–40. Boulder, CO: Lynne Rienner, 2002.

———. "Peace Processes and the Challenges of Violence." In *Contemporary Peacemaking: Conflict, Violence and Peace Processes*, edited by John Darby and Roger Mac Ginty, 103–13. London and New York: Palgrave Macmillan, 2003.

———. "Spoiler Problems in Peace Processes." *International Security* 22 (Fall 1997): 5–53.

Stedman, Stephen J., Donald Rothchild, and Elizabeth M. Cousens, eds. *Ending Civil Wars: The Implementation of Peace Agreements*. Boulder, CO: Lynne Rienner, 2002.

Straker, Gill, with Fatima Moosa, Rise Becker, and Madiyoyo Nkwale. *Faces in the Revolution: The Psychological Effect of Violence on Township Youth in South Africa*. Athens, OH: Ohio University Press, 1992.

Swaine, Aisling, with Thomas Feeny. "A Neglected Perspective: Adolescent Girls' Experiences of the Kosovo Conflict of 1999." In *Children and Youth on the Front Line: Ethnography, Armed Conflict, and Displacement*, edited by Jo Boyden and Joanna de Berry, 63–86. New York: Berghahn Books, 2004.

Tawil, Sobhi, and Alexandra Harley. *Education, Conflict and Social Cohesion*. Geneva: UNESCO International Bureau of Education, 2004.

Tawil, Sobhi, Alexandra Harley, and Lucy Porteous. *Curriculum Change and Social Cohesion in Conflict-Affected Societies*. Geneva: UNESCO, 2003.

Thompson, Carol. "Beyond Civil Society: Child Soldiers as Citizens in Mozambique." *Review of African Political Economy* 26 (June 1999): 191–206.

Tibbitts, Felisa. "Literature Review on Outcomes of School-Based Programs Related to 'Learning to Live Together.'" Geneva: UNESCO International Bureau of Education, January 2005.

Tolley, H. *Children and War: Political Socialization to International Conflict*. New York: Colombia University/Teachers College Press, 1973.

Truth and Reconciliation Commission of South Africa Report, 5 vols. Cape Town, South Africa: Juta Press, 1998.

United Nations Department of Economic and Social Affairs. *World Youth Report 2005*. New York: United Nations, October 2005. http://www.un.org/esa/socdev/unyin/wpayconflict.htm#WYR2005.

United Nations Office for the Coordination of Humanitarian Affairs. "Afghanistan: Eight Thousand Children under Arms Look for a Future." http://www.irinnews.org/webspecials/childsoldiers/Afghanistan031203. asp (accessed April 15, 2006).

United Nations Population Division. *World Population Prospects: The 2004 Revision.* Online database: http://esa.un.org/unpp/ (accessed May 21, 2006).

United Nations Secretary General. *Children and Armed Conflict.* Document A/59/695-S/2005/72, February 9, 2005. http://www.reliefweb.int/library/documents/2005/unsc-general-09feb.pdf.

United Nations Security Council. Resolution 1325 on Women, Peace and Security. http://www.peacewomen.org/un/sc/1325.html (accessed August 5, 2006).

United Nations Security Council. Resolution S/RES/1379 2001. 8(e), p. 3. Available at the Web site of the United Nations Office for the Coordination of Humanitarian Affairs. http://ochaonline.un.org/webpage.asp?Page=1790.

United Nations Security Council. "Security Council Establishes Monitoring, Reporting Mechanism on Use of Child Soldiers, Unanimously Adopting Resolution 1612 (2005)." Press Release SC/8458, July 26, 2005. http://www.un.org/News/Press/docs/2005/sc8458.doc.htm.

Urdal, Henrik. "The Devil in the Demographics: The Effect of Youth Bulges on Domestic Armed Conflict, 1950–2000." Social Development Papers, Conflict and Reconstruction Unit. Paper No. 14. Washington, DC: World Bank, July 2004.

U.S. Agency for International Development. "Youth and Conflict: A Toolkit for Intervention." Washington, DC: USAID, 2004.

Wallensteen, Peter, and Margareta Sollenberg. "Armed Conflict 1989–2000." *Journal of Peace Research* 38 (2001): 629–44.

Walter, Barbara F. "The Critical Barrier to Civil War Settlement." *International Organization* 51, no.3 (1997): 335–64.

Weiss, Taya. *Perpetrating Power: Small Arms in Post-Conflict Sierra Leone and Liberia.* Monograph No 116. Pretoria, South Africa: Institute for Security Studies, June 2005. http://www.iss.co.za/pubs/Monographs/N0116/Chap3.htm.

Wessells, Michael, and Davidson Jonah. "Recruitment and Reintegration of Former Youth Soldiers in Sierra Leone: Challenges of Reconciliation and Post-Accord Peace Building." In *Troublemakers or Peacemakers? Youth and Post-Accord Peace Building*, edited by Siobhán McEvoy-Levy, 27–48. Notre Dame, IN: University of Notre Dame Press, 2006.

Wolfensohn, James. "Remarks on Post-Conflict Peacebuilding at the United Nations Security Council, New York, NY, May 26, 2005." Available online at World Bank Web site.

World Bank. "Children and Youth: Areas of Intervention" Web page. Available online at World Bank Web site.

———. *Reshaping the Future: Education and Post Conflict Reconstruction*. Washington, DC: World Bank, 2005. http://www.eldis.org/static/DOC16511.htm.

Yamani, Mai. *Changed Identities: The Challenge of the New Generation in Saudi Arabia*. London: Royal Institute of International Affairs, 2000.

Zack-Williams, A. B. "Child Soldiers in the Civil War in Sierra Leone." *Review of African Political Economy* 28 (March 2001): 73–82.

Zahar, Marie Joelle. "Spoilers in Peace Processes: Voice, Exit, and Loyalty in the Post-Accord Period." In *Violence and Reconstruction*, edited by John Darby, 33–52. Notre Dame, IN: University of Notre Dame Press, 2006.

Zartman, I. William. *Ripe for Resolution: Conflict and Intervention in Africa*. New Haven, CT: Yale University Press, 1989.

Ziv, A., A. W. Kruglanski, and S. Schulman. "Children's Psychological Reactions to Wartime Stress." *Journal of Personality and Social Psychology* 30 (1974): 24–30.

Lightning Source UK Ltd.
Milton Keynes UK
UKHW020002230621
385978UK00007B/142